HANDLING *the* TRUTH

HANDLING
the
TRUTH

On the Writing of Memoir

BETH KEPHART

For Terri:

Who hope such enthuse
to her world of work
& books.

GOTHAM BOOKS

GOTHAM BOOKS
Published by the Penguin Group
Penguin Group (USA) Inc., 375 Hudson Street,
New York, New York 10014, USA

USA | Canada | UK | Ireland | Australia
New Zealand | India | South Africa | China
Penguin Books Ltd, Registered Offices:
80 Strand, London WC2R 0RL, England
For more information about the Penguin Group visit penguin.com.

LIBRARY OF CONGRESS CATALOGING-IN-PUBLICATION DATA
Kephart, Beth.
  Handling the truth : on the writing of memoir / Beth Kephart.
    pages cm
  ISBN 978-1-592-40815-3
  1. Autobiography—Authorship.   2. Biography as a literary
form.   I. Title.
  CT25.K37 2013
  808.06'692—dc23   2012043517

Printed in the United States of America
10 9 8 7 6 5 4 3

Set in Bembo
Designed by Spring Hoteling

for my students—essential, inspiriting, whole-making
for Amy Rennert, who was sure

CONTENTS

INTRODUCTION

Throughout the 1990s, I was an unknown and in many ways unschooled writer who was deeply in love with her son. Love, for me, was the time I sat with this boy reading stories. It was the songs I sang to him at night. It was the walks we took and the hats we bought and the important things he taught me about language both received and given, and courage made essential. I wrote love one fragment at a time. I webbed it together until discrete essays became a binding narrative. I sent the manuscript out, a slush-pile writer. When this small book of mine—a family book, an intimate book—found readers beyond people I personally knew, I was utterly unprepared. I had been an outsider. I had written from the margins. I still had much to learn.

I would go on to write four more memoirs and a river book that I called *Flow* that assumed the memoir's form. I would be asked to conduct workshops and give talks—in elementary schools, in middle schools, in high schools, at universities, in libraries and community centers. I would write about the writing life for publications great and small. I would chair juries for the National Book Awards and the PEN First Nonfiction Awards and serve on a jury panel for the National Endowment for the Arts. I would explore new genres—poetry, fable, young adult literature. I would—a brave experiment—begin to blog daily in memoiristic fashion. The important thing to me was this: I was still writing. I was still reading. I was still learning.

When the University of Pennsylvania asked me to teach creative nonfiction, I was not inclined to say yes. Raised up in memoir on my own, surrounded by my own huge but idiosyncratic memoir library, still in many ways making my outsider way into the book world, it wasn't at all clear to me that I would succeed within an Ivy League environment among faculty members who knew what teaching was. I hadn't grown up in the workshop system; how could I teach it? With the exception of three ten-day summer programs I enrolled in when I was already a mother, I had never taken a formal writing class. I was the true memoir autodidact, and this was Penn, where, as a student years before, I had studied the history and sociology of science, swerving clear of English.

As it turns out, teaching at Penn had been my calling all along. I eased into the responsibility—first mentoring a single student, then teaching a select advanced class, then taking on the teaching of Creative Nonfiction 135.302, which has become my favorite job of all. In teaching others memoir, I have taught it to myself—the language of expectations and critique, the exemplary work of others, the exercises that yield well-considered work, the morality of the business, the psychic cautions. Teaching memoir is teaching vulnerability is teaching voice is teaching self. Next to motherhood, it has been, for me, the greatest privilege.

It has also—perhaps inevitably—led to the writing of

this book. *Handling the Truth* is about the making of memoir, and the consequences. It's about why so many get it wrong, and about how to get it right. It's about the big questions: Is compassion teachable? Do half memories count? Are landscape, weather, color, taste, and music background or foreground? To whom does *then* belong? And what rights do memoirists have, and how does one transcend particulars to achieve a universal tale, and how does a memoirist feel, once the label is attached, and what *is* the language of truth? *Handling the Truth* is about knowing ourselves. It's about writing, word after word, and if it swaggers a little, I hope it teaches a lot, providing a proven framework for teachers, students, and readers.

ONE

DEFINITIONS, PRELIMINARIES, CAUTIONS

PREFATORY

MAYBE the audacity of it thrills you. Maybe it's always been like this: You out on the edge with your verity serums, your odd-sized heart, your wet eyes, urging. Maybe this is what you are good for, after all, or good *at*, though there, you've done it again: wanted proof, suggested the possibility. You teach memoir. You negotiate truth. Goodness doesn't matter here. Bearing witness does.

Memoir is a strut and a confession, a whisper in the ear, a scream. Memoir performs, then cedes. It is the work of thieves. It is a seduction and a sleight of hand, and the world won't rise above it.

Or you won't. You in the Victorian manse at the edge of the Ivy League campus, where you arrive early and sit in the attitude of prayer. You who know something not just of the toil but also of the psychic cost, the pummeling doubt, the lacerating regrets that live in the aftermath of public confession. You have written memoir in search of the lessons children teach and in confusion over the entanglements of friendships. You have written in despair regarding the sensational impossibility of knowing another, in defense of the imperiled imagination, and in the throes of the lonesome sink toward middle age. You have written quiet and expected quiet, and yet a terrible noise has hurried in—a churlish self-recrimination that cluttered the early hours when clear-minded nonmemoirists slept. You have learned from all that. You have decided. Memoir is, and will still be, but cautions must be taken.

Teaching memoir is teaching verge. It's teaching questions: Who are you? Where have you been? Where are you going? What do you believe in? What will you fight for? What is the sound of your voice? It's teaching *now* against *then*, and leave that out to put this in, and yes, maybe that happened, but what does it *mean*? An affront? You hope not. A calling? Probably.

You enter a classroom of students you have never seen before, and over the course of a semester you travel—their forgotten paraphernalia in the well of their backpacks, those tattoos on their wrists, those bio notes inked onto the palm of one hand. They will remember their mother's London broil, but not the recipe. They will proffer a profusion of umbrellas and a poor-fitting snowsuit, a pair of polka-dotted boots, red roses at a Pakistani grave, a white billiard ball, a pink-and-orange sari, a box with a secret bottom, Ciao Bella gelato. Someone will make a rat-a-tat out of a remembered list. Someone will walk you through the corridors of the sick or through the staged room of a movie set or beside the big bike that will take them far. Someone will say, *Teach me how to write like this*, and someone will ask what good writing is, and you will read out loud from the memoirs you have loved, debunk (systematically) and proselytize (effusively), perform Patti Smith and Terrence Des Pres, Geoffrey Wolff and Mark Richard, Marie Arana and Mary Karr,

William Fiennes and Michael Ondaatje, C. K. Williams and Natalie Kusz. You will play recordings of Sylvia Plath reciting "Lady Lazarus" and Etheridge Knight intoning "The Idea of Ancestry," and you will say, in a room made dark by encrusted velvet and mahogany stain, *You tell me good. You tell me why. Know your opinions and defend them.*

These aspiring makers of memoir are who you believe and what you believe in—the smiley face tie he wears on Frat Rush Tuesdays, the cheerful interval between her two front teeth, the planks he carries in his dark-blue backpack, the accoutrements of power lifting. Enamored of the color red and hip-hop, declaring you their "galentine," impersonating Whitman, missing their mothers, missing their dead, they are, simply and complexly, human, and they may not trust themselves with truth, but they have to trust one another. You insist that they earn the trust of one another.

And so you will send them out into the world with cameras. And so you will sit them down with songs. And so you will ask them to retrieve what they lost and, after that, to leave aside the merely incidental. You will set a box of cookies on the table, some chocolate-covered berries, some salt-encrusted chips, and then (at last) get out of the way, for every memoir must in the end and on its own emerge and bleed and scab.

Audacity was the wrong word; you see that now. The word, in fact, is *privilege*. Teaching, after all these years, is the marrow in your bones. Truth is your obsession.

MEMOIR IS NOT

HERE are some of the things that memoir is not:

- A chronological, thematically tone-deaf recitation of everything remembered. That's autobiography, which should be left, in this twenty-first century, to politicians and celebrities. Oh, be honest: It should just be left.

- A typeset version of a diary scrawl—unfiltered, unshaped. There are remarkable diaries; *A Woman in Berlin* (anonymous), for example, is artful, heart-breaking, essential. *New York Diaries: 1609 to 2009* (Teresa Carpenter, editor) is a thrill. But the method of a diarist is to record events and thoughts *as they are happening*. A memoirist looks back.

- Exhibitionism for exhibitionism's sake. If nothing's been learned from a life, is it worth sharing? Or, if nothing's been learned *yet*, shouldn't the story wait?

- An accusation, a retaliation, a big *take that!* in type. Fights are waged in bedrooms and courthouses. A memoir is not a fight.

- A lecture, a lesson, a stew of information and facts. Memoirs illuminate and reveal, as opposed to justify and record. They connote and suggest but never insist.

- A self-administered therapy session. Memoirists speak to others and not just to themselves.

- An exercise in self-glorification; an ability—or refusal—to accept one's own culpability; a false allegiance to the idea that a life, any life, can be perfectly lived or faultlessly explained.

- An unwillingness to recognize—either explicitly or implicitly—that memory is neither machine nor uncontestable. Memory—our own and others'—is a tricky, fallible business.

- A trumped-up, fantastical idea of what an interesting life might have been, *if only*. A web of lies. A smudge. A mockery of reality. There is a separate (even equal) category for such things. It goes by the name of fiction.

MEMOIR IS

IF you want to write memoir, you need to set caterwaul-
ing narcissism to the side. You need to soften your stance.
You need to work through the explosives—anger, aggran-
dizement, injustice, misfortune, despair, fumes—toward
mercy. Real memoirists, *literary* memoirists, don't justify be-
haviors, decisions, moods. They don't ladder themselves
up—high, high, high—so as to look down upon the rest of
us. Real memoirists open themselves to self-discovery and,
in the process, make themselves vulnerable—not just to the
world but also to themselves. They yearn, and they are
yearned with. They declare a want to know. They seek out
loud. They quest. They lessen the distance. They lean
toward.

Listen, for example, to Michael Ondaatje as he sets out
to rediscover—and make sense of—his Sri Lankan childhood. From the opening pages of *Running in the Family*:

> I had already planned the journey back. During
> quiet afternoons I spread maps onto the floor and
> searched out possible routes to Ceylon. But it was
> only in the midst of this party, among my closest

friends, that I realized I would be travelling back to the family I had grown from—those relations from my parents' generation who stood in my memory like frozen opera. I wanted to touch them into words. A perverse and solitary desire. In Jane Austen's *Persuasion* I had come across the lines, "she had been forced into prudence in her youth—she learned romance as she grew older—the natural sequence of an unnatural beginning." In my midthirties I realized I had slipped past a childhood I had ignored and not understood.

Diane Keaton, a celebrity who wrote not autobiography but memoir with *Then Again*, uses collage (letters written, journals plumbed, secrets exposed) to parse a question and to explore (beautifully, calmly, as a human being and not as a star) a thoughtfully articulated theme. It's all here in a single sentence—hardly easy gloss. It's the crinkly stuff of living and losing, and it sets the book in motion:

> Comparing two women with big dreams who shared many of the same conflicts and also happened to be mother and daughter is partially a story of what's lost in success contrasted with what's gained in accepting an ordinary life.

Maybe memoir, for some, is the Queen of the Nasties—the medical horror story, the impossible loss story, the abuse story, the deprivation story, the I've-been-cheated story, the headline-making *you're kidding me*s. But plot (which is to say the stuff of a life) is empty if it doesn't signify, and the unexamined tragedy—thank you, Socrates—isn't worth the trees it will be inked on or the screen that fingers will smudge. Some of the best memoirs are built not from sensate titillations but from the contemplation of universal questions within a framed perspective.

Annie Dillard, for example, is not a victim in her growing-up classic, *An American Childhood*. She's a woman looking back on what it meant to grow awake to the world.

> I woke in bits, like all children, piecemeal over the years. I discovered myself and the world, and forgot them, and discovered them again. I woke at intervals until, by that September when Father went down the river, the intervals of waking tipped the scales, and I was more often awake than not. I noticed this process of waking, and predicted with terrifying logic that one of these years not far away I would be awake continuously and never slip back, and never be free of myself again.

Likewise, while loss frames C. K. Williams's *Misgivings*, it's not the tragedy he's chasing. It's understanding.

> My father dead, I come into the room where he lies and I say aloud, immediately concerned that he might still be able to hear me, *What a war we had!* To my father's body I say it, still propped up on its pillows, before the men from the funeral home arrive to put him into their horrid zippered green bag to take him away, before his night table is cleared of the empty bottles of pills he wolfed down when

he'd finally been allowed to end the indignity of his suffering, and had found the means to do it. Before my mother comes in to lie down beside him.

When my mother dies, I'll say to her, as unexpectedly, knowing as little that I'm going to, "I love you." But to my father, again now, my voice, as though of its own accord, blurts, *What a war!* And I wonder again why I'd say that. It's been years since my father and I raged at each other the way we once did, violently, rancorously, seeming to loathe, despise, detest one another. Years since we'd learned, perhaps from each other, perhaps each in our struggles with ourselves, that conflict didn't have to be as it had been for so long the routine state of affairs between us.

In *Father's Day*, Buzz Bissinger is in keen pursuit of understanding, too, though in this memoir about raising twin sons, one of whom suffers irreparable brain damage at birth, it's Bissinger's own inability to be at peace, to find solace, to be *okay* that generates the tension, and the search.

It is strange to love someone so much who is still so fundamentally mysterious to you after all these years. *Strange* is a lousy word, meaning nothing. It is the most terrible pain of my life. As much as I try to engage Zach, figure out how to make the flower germinate because there is a seed, I also run. I run out of guilt. I run because he was robbed and I feel I was robbed. I run because of my shame. I am not proud to feel or say this. But I think these things, not all the time, but too many times, which only increases the cycle of my shame. This is *my* child. How can I look at him this way?

Marie Arana wrote *American Chica* not to exploit a family or to out dark secrets, not to trump or to claim, but to somehow register how two exceptionally different people—her parents—could sustain a home.

A South American man, a North American woman—hoping against hope, throwing a frail span over the divide, trying to bolt beams into sand. There was one large lesson they had yet to learn as they strode into the garden with friends, hungry from rum and fried blood: There is a fundamental rift between North and South America, a flaw so deep it is tectonic. The plates don't fit. The earth is loose. A fault runs through. Earthquakes happen. Walls are likely to fall.

As I looked down at their fleeting radiance, I had no idea I would spend the rest of my life puzzling over them.

And then there's Jeanette Winterson, in *Why Be Happy When You Could Be Normal?*. She is writing not to abrade her mother—she might have, the material was there—but to report back out from a life of searching on the matter and the necessity of love.

Listen, we are human beings. Listen, we are inclined to love. Love is there, but we need to be taught how. We want to stand upright, we want to walk, but someone needs to hold our hand and balance us a bit, and guide us a bit, and scoop us up when we fall.

Listen, we fall. Love is there but we have to learn it—and its shapes and its possibilities. I taught myself to stand on my own two feet, but I could not teach myself how to love.

Beauty is born of urgency; that should be clear. Forced knowing is false knowing—self-evident, perhaps? Voice is tone and mood and attitude, and tense will make a difference. Makers of memoir shape what they have lived and what they have seen. They honor what they love and defend what they believe. They dwell with ideas and language and with themselves, countering complexity with clarity and manipulating (for the sake of seeing) time. They locate stories inside the contradictions of their lives—the false starts and the presumed victories, the epiphanies that rub themselves raw nearly as soon as they are stated. They write the stories once; they write them several times.

They take a breath.

They sing.

And when their voices are true, we hear them true. We trust them.

READ TO WRITE

ONCE I had a friend. Yes. Once. It had occurred to her to write a book, a memoir in particular, and so she called, asking for help. *It should be fun*, she said. I set to work creating a list of the memoirs my friend might read, for she hadn't read even so much as a single memoir yet, and I thought reading might be helpful. I sent the list and that was that— the end of the memoir, and of the friendship.

I don't mean to be insulting when I suggest that memoir writers should read memoir, but there they are—my annoying politics. Stories live inside the pages of memoirs, but so do strategies, tactics. Fine little experiments with points of view and tense. Daring reversals of structure. Elisions and white space. Italics pressed up against roman. I'm a little bit sorry, but the facts are the facts: You have to read memoir to write it.

I read in the earliest part of the day—before my husband stirs, before the glisten on the grass burns off, before anybody anywhere can suggest a different agenda. I read outside on the old chaise longue, or on the slatted, sloping deck, or on my side of the bed, turned toward the breeze and the clean pink morning light.

Reading is equally about exiting and entering, about going away and going nowhere. Reading early in the morning is like having one more dream, like lolling just a little longer in the strange, sweet gauze of sleep. If I were to draw myself in the morning reading, I would draw my head as a cloud—edgeless and capacious and shape-shifting and un-bound, hovering near but never tethered to the bones and muscles of my body. I read, I am saying, and without moving anywhere I go—into the deep, wild, sometimes contradicting, mostly illuminating language and landscape of memoir. I learn (over and again) how memoir is made. I learn what memoirists teach.

With *Road Song*, Natalie Kusz teaches the importance of selecting just the right details, and of giving them room on the page. With *Running in the Family*, Michael Ondaatje commends the power of fragments and the integrity of not being entirely sure—or sane. With *Half a Life*, Darin Strauss teaches white space. With *House of Prayer No. 2*, Mark Richard teaches intimate second-person prose. With *Just Kids*, Patti Smith teaches how much room memoir can make to preserve the integrity (and privacy) of others. With *The Duke of Deception*, Geoffrey Wolff teaches forgiveness. With *Bone Black*, bell hooks teaches the power of the returning refrain.

The good memoirs aren't just good stories. They are instructions on both life and form, considerations of shapes, shadows thrown up onto the wall. They are—they must be—works of art. It's fundamental, then, isn't it? You have to know what art is before you set out to write it. You have to have a dictionary of working terms, a means by which you can deliver up a verdict on your own sentences and their arrangements.

Buy the books. (There's an appendix back there to get you started.) Increase your shelf space. Go dirty and dog-eared; take an afternoon sprawl. "When you find only yourself interesting, you're boring," Grace Paley said. "True memoir is written, like all literature, in an attempt to find not only a self but a world," Patricia Hampl said.

Don't be boring.

Find the world.

And then (and only then) wedge yourself within it.

GREAT EXPECTATIONS

IN the faces of my students I see the person I once was, though I was nearly twice their age, married, and a mother when I enrolled in my first writers' workshop. We'd flown to Spoleto, Italy, for a family vacation, and we'd climbed hills and slipped inside churches and sat beneath rooms where pianos were playing. There were nuns on the hills, ropes at their waists. There were market flowers wilted by sun. We'd arrived late at night and settled into a stranger's flat (the plates still draining by the kitchen sink, a cloud of smoky moon in the front window), and the next day I'd hauled myself up the stairs of a round-cornered building and sat in the back of the class.

I'd brought a blank book with gray pages, its cover hieroglyphically embossed. I'd read the works of our teachers, Reginald Gibbons and Rosellen Brown, and beyond the window, deep in the hills, was the Roman theater and the turreted castle, the Cathedral of Santa Maria Assunta, the shop of silver trinkets and cards from which my toddler son would soon (almost) catastrophically run as a Fiat hurtled by. The poisonous wasp that would balloon my husband's hand was out there. The pizza shop with the festoon of paper flowers at the base of the hill. The slinking arm of the aqueduct. The basilica in pale light, its beauty explained by my husband with two words: *forced perspective.* The cemetery where soon the class would go to imagine the lives of those whose names we'd find scratched out of headstones and buffed by a woman bearing (in broad daylight) a candle flame and a white handkerchief.

But at that moment there was only the classroom, the squeak-footed chairs, my blank book, the other students, Rosellen, and Reginald, and it was Reginald who began: "Every difference makes a difference." Word for word, I transcribed him. "The craft of writing is to describe something so that someone else can see it." Soon Reginald was quoting Henry James—"Be one of those on whom nothing is lost"—and then Rosellen was speaking: "I like the sentence that begins romantically, then de-romanticizes itself."

The sentence that de-romanticizes itself.

I had been a closet writer nearly all my life—my poems stuffed in boxes, my short stories boomeranged back to me via return-envelope mail. I was taking my first lesson in craft, and what I learned in Spoleto, what I chose to value or come to believe about myself, would shape the way I thought about stories made and lived every thereafter day of my life. It would make me want to find a way to pass the knowing down.

Spoleto also began for me the process of examining, defining, and attempting to live up to my own literary expectations. What was I looking for in the writers I read? What was I hoping for from myself? Why hadn't I asked myself these questions before? Why had I left so much to hazy qualifiers? Why did I not yet have a standard that I was holding myself to? What does *good* mean, after all? And what did I mean, when I said, simply, *I love it?*

Things had to change.

They did.

Of memoirists—I have learned as I have read, learned as I have taught, learned as I have reviewed my own work and the work of others—I expect deliberation with structure, ambition with language, compassion in tone, magnanimous reach, a refusal to presume that chronology alone teaches. And since I am so busy expecting that of others, I cop to expecting it of myself. Memoirs—their memoirs, my memoirs—must transcend not just the category and the particulars of the story but also, ultimately, the author herself.

My expectations, then. But what about yours? What about the expectations of my students? In that Victorian manse on the edge of my campus, extraordinary work emerges when I give my students 750 words each to express their expectations. The prompt question may seem simple enough: *What do you expect of others as you read, and what do you expect of yourself as a writer?* The responses, however, have been remarkable, establishing for each writer not just a critical vocabulary and frame but also a contract of sorts. *This is what I'm looking for,* each essay concludes, in its own fashion. *Look at me setting the bar.*

I rarely know what to expect of my students' expectations essays. I have never—and this is deeply true—been disappointed. The essay fragments that I share here are meant to inspire you. Who am I kidding? They absolutely inspire me.

I expect, in a well-written piece, to be drawn in without my notice. I don't want awkwardly chosen words to fight for my attention. I want the attraction to feel effortless and instant, as if the writer doesn't even know she's being read. Or, even further: I want to imagine that a piece of writing is just an elegant, authorless, whole thought that had already existed before a writer nets it onto a page. Part of my fantasy is that the writer does not even care if the piece is read; this autonomous thing on the page is just fanning its wings and sunning itself, wholly innocent of me, the reader-voyeur. The writer is someone who has carelessly left a pair of glasses on the grass so that I can have a look. —Sara

Address me (first-person point-of-views are a good way to start, but not necessary) and acknowledge my presence. I want to know that you're writing for someone other than yourself: me. Write with intentionality. Labor over every sentence and every other word. Because at night, when I hold these bound pages you regard as your life's work, I want to read it with the trust that you have thought long and hard about the impact of your words on my mind. Because when I arrive at the destination your words have brought me to, I want to know that my journey is the result of your love. —Rachel

I hold the writers I read to the same standards as I hold myself. I enjoy writing that feels genuine because it allows me to trust the author and become more invested in his or her work. When I encounter writing that is pretentious or condescending, I put up a barrier that prevents me from getting anything out of the work at all. I get a great deal more out of reading when authors use imagery and description to draw me into their story and make it come alive. —Nabil

I also expect compassion for the people mentioned in a piece. We are all fallible and faulted. I expect fairness in a portrayal; very few people are flat characters, merely good or bad. Geoffrey Wolff's *The Duke of Deception* was a great example of compassion. Though his father was a fraud, he still can say, "I had this from him always: compassion, care, generosity, and endurance." Another aspect of fairness is consideration of others' vulnerability: throughout our lives, others entrust us with their secrets. I wouldn't default on that trust without explicit permission. Not everything we know about the people in our lives is fair game. I want to be respectful of others in my writing. —Erin

What, then, is the stimulus for entertainment? Reading appeals to people from a voyeuristic perspective—the contrived intimacy of knowing others blithely and truly, with no repercussions, is the consummation of high human fantasy. We long for social connection at will. The mentioned aspects of literary entertainment entice the

reader for their functional relationship to the voyeur's fulfillment: they simulate the closeness and familiarity while belying the actual vacuum between reader and character. In his essay, Seabrook shows us Schnabel the way his visitors see him—or the way that they might. The legitimacy of the reader's depiction is unimportant and personal—the facts that paint that picture remain true. DeLillo's encomia to contemporary commercialism and the academy place us in the confused mind of an intellectual, bridging conceptions with shifting tones, allowing the narrative to speak as much implicitly as it does explicitly. This is what I expect in writing, and what I expect to give.
—Jonathan

Once I am committed to a book, I want to feel as though I am in an unhealthy serious relationship, the kind where you don't ever want to go anywhere without the significant other and it's all that is on your mind. I like to be able to know and empathize with the characters, so I can talk about them as if I were gossiping about a friend. While I can appreciate a poetic writer that crafts beautifully poised sentences, I tend to be more attracted to raw and honest writing, someone who can tell a good story without sounding pretentious. A good ending is pivotal; this doesn't mean every story has to have a fairy tale ending, but as I've learned in psychology, the "recency effect" claims that I'm most likely going to remember the last part I read.

Thus a writer should want to leave the reader with anything but an inadequate closure; lingering questions are acceptable, but a weak and poorly cohesive conclusion will only leave a sour taste in my mouth. —Katie

I expect myself to surprise my reader by endowing my piece with that certain X factor that transforms a memory into a story. I want to do this on the linguistic level, by varying my sentence length and experimenting with punctuation (I find the dash to be very powerful when used correctly). Perhaps more importantly, I expect to surprise myself (or maybe I don't *expect* this, because then it wouldn't be quite a surprise). But I can and do expect myself to be open to the possibility of surprise, and not to confine my memoir to a given framework within which it has no room to develop. I am excited to see how my writing and my voice will emerge. —Leah

From writers, I expect consideration for their readers, a balance of meaningful details, and a sense of destination for their own writing. I look for a certain kind of pensiveness and perceptiveness in writers that I rarely expect from normal people. I want writers who always ask "Why?" or "What is this, *really*?" and labor to figure it out. They know what they're looking for, and they take the readers with them on their search. Thinking about memoir, the importance of a mission, a framework is becoming so clear to me. We all have endless stories; our lives are impossible to summarize, and we shouldn't try! Writers should be able to parse out the golden threads from their own writing, know what to keep and what to scrap, and organize it all with the reader, and their own destination in mind. I also definitely expect writers to know *how to read*. —Andrea

Here then, after reading, is your first assignment. Know, for yourself, what draws you to the memoirs that you read. Know what you expect of you. Write it down and keep it close. Don't fail your own gold standards.

CAREFUL, NOW

BEING out in the world with books of my own, I know the price of advice. I know the urgency behind the questions: *Read me? Teach me? Love me? Make me a writer?* When you lean in the direction of another's work, you lean precariously out of your own. When you attend to the dreams and works of others, you are thrown from the path you had been on. Teaching is a succession of invasions and beginnings. And yet, of course, I lean.

But in reminding others to keep their hearts open, I remind myself. In teaching respect, I keep myself in check. When I recite the words of poet-novelist Forrest Gander—"Maybe the best we can do is try to leave ourselves unprotected . . ."—I wear my jacket just a little less snug on the long walk home. When I recite Edith Wharton—"One good heart-break will furnish the poet with many songs, and the novelist with a considerable number of novels. But they must have hearts that can break."—I ask myself, *At my old age, is my heart still capable of breaking?*

I am right there with my students as I teach my students, I'm saying. Whenever I teach memoir, when I contemplate it, when I have the urge to again write it, I live in the danger zone.

It's obvious, isn't it? Memoir making is a hazardous business. People are involved. Their feelings. Their reputations. Their relationships to you. Put somebody into a book you write, and you have changed—forever—the equation. I teach this to others. I teach it to myself. Over and over again.

Careful, now, I say. To them. To myself. Because it doesn't matter if you think your portraits flatter. It doesn't matter if you think the jokes are on you. It doesn't matter if you tag another as hero and escalate the praise. None of it matters. Memoir writers have no control over how their cast of characters—which is to say their mothers, their fathers, their siblings, their cousins, their early friends and late friends, their ancient lovers, their current partners, their neighbors, their teammates, their colleagues, their professors, their students, their children—will feel about what has taken up residency on your page. Call someone nice in a memoir and maybe she'll think you're chastising her as a bore. Accuse another of a kindness, and he may well think you've not paid homage to the thing that mattered more. Overtly accuse or overtly divulge, and it might—no, it will—get bloody. The war could last for years. The war could be unending.

And do not forget this. Learn it from me. People grow up. Children do. Memoirs freeze people in time. Sometimes that isn't the most loving thing to do. Others may forgive you, but will you forgive yourself?

Memoir making, the myth goes, is tenderness reserved for the book, intelligence transferred to the page, generosity given over to scene. But it is also, obviously, grand larceny, a form of plagiarism, a brand of stalking, and those who teach memoir have, I think, a moral responsibility to steady the student with terms, to caution her about consequences, to insist that he do it again, better, until the structure is solid and right, until the memoir can stand up against the ammunition hidden in the tall grass on the other side of the wall. Memoir making in the classroom is not a vanity operation. It is about melding the eye and the *I* into something that actually matters—yes—while at the same time talking through the messiness of life. It's about giving the writer room to know himself, while making it clear (very clear) that those we have loved or warred against or not forgotten may be very happy living outside the public's big-eyed glare, thank you very much.

Real writers, I have said throughout these many years, do not write to trump or abolish. They write, instead, to rumble or howl, or because language is salvation, or because they've been alive, or because they have survived, or because they are determined to survive, tomorrow and the next day. Write for the right reasons, I implore. Write real. Write with the understanding, as Erin wrote in her expectations essay, that some lives or secrets do not belong to us. Write knowing that there are those who will inevitably walk away, and after that, there are those who will mock the form, who will dangle out their suspicions, who will attach the term *memoir* (which has its roots in French and evokes *reminisce*) to the meanest list of accusations.

Memoir is lesser, you will read. Memoir is suspiciously easy. Consider Daniel Mendelsohn, writing in *The New Yorker*, who proffered this "sounds like/looks like" list of labels for the genre: "unseemly self-exposures, unpalatable betrayals, unavoidable mendacity, a soupçon of meretriciousness." Consider Ben Yagoda's *Memoir: A History*, where we learn that "memoir is to fiction as photography is to painting, also, in being easier to do fairly well. Only a master can create a convincing and compelling fictional world. Anyone with a moderate level of discipline, insight, intelligence, and editorial skill—plus a more than moderately interesting life—can write a decent memoir."

You might feel better after your memoir is written, in other words. But after it is read, after the critics have had their say, after you have overheard your neighbors at the block party whispering, after your sister has rebuked your way of remembering, how will you feel?

Be prepared. Be cognizant. Move forward, but with caution.

TWO

RAW MATERIAL

WRESTLING
YOURSELF DOWN

DICTION, the poet Mary Oliver says, is the atmosphere created by word choices—the sound of those words, their relative precision, their various and variant connotations.

The atmosphere created by words. Yes. Write memoir, and you are writing atmosphere.

But what *kind*, exactly? Do you know? Do you know who you are, what you are capable of, how what you *choose* to see speaks of who you are? Do you know what mood you leave behind, or could? Do you know what trembles in your wake, and what might turn its back on you? Are you lazy, jiving, elaborate, prepossessing, imagistic, postmodern, slaying, friendly, intricate, intimate on the page? Is your speaking voice like your memoir voice? How many personae can you fit inside your hat? How is persona not in itself a lie? Why is thinking about all this—and thinking about it early—so very necessary?

It's necessary because the indiscriminate *I* is haphazard and poorly informed. It is often dull and deselective. It does not qualify, as Ander Monson writes in "Voir Dire," as art: "I guess I want awareness," Monson says, "a sense that the writer has reckoned with the self, the material, as well as what it means to reveal it, and how secrets are revealed, how stories are told, that it's not just being simply told. In short, it must make something of itself."

Yes, of course. But how?

Start small, I advise. Don't try to write The Memoir straight off; don't attack it heart first and head strong. You'll get lost in its bigness, its tufted landscapes, its endless contradictions, its minor and major assaults. You'll lose your way, or you'll lose your opportunity. Start small by making notes to yourself. Go out and buy yourself a blank-page journal. Prose poem your days. Launch a blog. Write about what is happening right now so that you can learn to write well about what happened yesterday.

The following three passages are all excerpted from *New York Diaries: 1609 to 2009*. Here, outside the confines of formal memoir, are writers observing the world around them—and experimenting with voice. Clouds are "exactly parallel to avenues." People are "prematurely uglied." A man smokes "volcanically." Not one of these diarists is merely recording the facts. The facts are being inhabited, transfigured. These sentences, to borrow from Monson, are making something of themselves:

> this evening 2 (uptown): long strings of cirrus clouds are sparkling electric fire orange against a still-blue sky, the same calm attention, the clouds are exactly parallel to avenues, and i smile and tear in relief: the city is in the sky again, dazzled, i'm stunned by natural beauty for the first time all week, the second-nature beauty of my city

moving again in time. —Chad the Minx, September 17, 2001

At the Warwick Hotel in a room full of crones for a movie. A collection of age and failure. I among them, prematurely uglied, am cast as an extra in a film I don't even know the name of. —Judith Malina, July 17, 1956

I was indefatigable this morning and tonight I stayed quietly at home, smoked volcanically, and read Burns, of whose writings I ought to know more than I do. —George Templeton Strong, January 6, 1842

Journal keeping, diary making, blogging—it's all a curious thing, and it isn't (I'll make the point again) memoir. But it's a start, an inroad, a gesture. It tells us something about ourselves, records the details of our living, puts dialogue somewhere safe so that we can retrieve it later, talks back to us about us. When I ask my students to journal daily, I ask them not to judge and not to filter. Just put it down, I say—whatever you think of, however you want. A week goes by, and I send along a copy of Joan Didion's short, classic essay "On Keeping a Notebook." Write three paragraphs about the notebook pages that you have been keeping, I say. What is the value of the notes you have kept? What did they teach you about yourself? How honest are the pages, and what do you expect they will mean to you ten or twenty years from now? What shouts back at you about your voice and the sentences you leave behind?

Joe, one of what has become a succession of supremely talented engineering students, discovered this:

I'm a fairly logical person, and my brain tends to move through a series of conclusions faster than I can control. This "quick thinking" is generally considered an asset. But speeding down a road makes it mighty hard to turn down any of the side streets or see what's outside the window. Writing down my thoughts forced my mind to spin its tires, bogged down by the physical limit of my writing speed. But by taking my time, and exploring many different options at each stage, I came to much more significant conclusions. In one case—Friday, I believe—I threw around a problem that had been frustrating me for a while. It seemed to be an impossible dilemma: how could my morally upstanding friend enjoy the college social life without compromising his integrity? I'd run it through a hundred times and was convinced it was a flaw in our society. It wouldn't be the first, after all. But then, in writing my assigned notebook entry, I articulated the problem in a few different ways. Looking at it in a different light, I realized that it would not necessarily be a compromise of his integrity, but rather a stage of growth and change. If there was anything holding him back, it was just as much pride as it was "integrity." To say that I totally changed my opinion would be an exaggeration, but I certainly have a new feeling towards the problem. Thanks to the notebook, I was driving slow enough to see it.

Notebook keeping seems an awkward exercise to some, but much is learned. What were they doing, the students ask me, ask themselves, obsessing so much about food? Why were they having trouble telling the truth? Why did they write in half sentences or in bullets or in the margins correcting themselves—for the sake of whom, exactly? Are they as anxious as they seem? Will they really never stop remembering that girlfriend? Why do they sit in the same exact chair every single evening?

And do they really sound like that?

Sound like what? I ask in class, and they begin, they self-diagnose, they express surprise:

> *I'm more matter-of-fact than I thought I was.*
>
> *I'm more secretive.*
>
> *I'm too trapped in my head.*
>
> *I write about being anxious without saying why I'm anxious.*
>
> *I've got to lighten up.*
>
> *Maybe I'm not the poet I thought I was.*
>
> *I swear I've got to stop thinking about food.*
>
> *I need to stop sounding like her.*
>
> *My sentences go nowhere.*
>
> *There's not an original metaphor in twenty pages.*

There is the who they thought they were and the who they wrote down, the something lost and the something gained, the discrepancy, now easily measured, between the voice they hear in their heads and the voice they find on their paper. "Our notebooks give us away," Joan Didion observes. And they do. They also provide, to memoir makers, a shelf and a foundation, as she goes on to observe.

> I think we are well advised to keep on nodding terms with the people we used to be, whether we find them attractive company or not. Otherwise they turn up unannounced and surprise us, come hammering on the mind's door at 4 a.m. of a bad night and demand to know who deserted them, who betrayed them, who is going to make amends. We forget all too soon the things we thought we could never forget. We forget the loves and the betrayals alike, forget what we whispered and what we screamed, forget who we were.

So keep a notebook, and take note. Use obsessions and anxieties to your advantage, plumb the details for metaphor, negotiate the distance between the story you have to tell and the voice with which you can tell it, and above all else, know yourself. Maybe there's work to do in aligning your ideas with your sound. Maybe tweeting all day has curbed your capacity for expansion. Maybe you need to let down the guard on your jokey self because there's only so far that funny can go; at some point funny goes hollow if it doesn't add up to more, if there isn't a visible soul behind the pranks. Maybe you, like Alison Bechdel in her graphic memoir *Fun Home*, will need some time to figure out whether even your private, right-now words are true. In the following scene, Bechdel is depicting herself at work on her own teenage journal. She's up against the memoirist's dilemma.

> It was a sort of epistemological crisis. How did I know that the things I was writing were absolutely, objectively true? My simple, declarative sentences began to strike me as hubristic at best, utter lies at worst. All I could speak for was my own perceptions, and perhaps not even those.

A journal is written so that a journal might be studied. A journal is where the work-in-progress writer begins to wrestle his- or herself down, begins to understand or tussle with his or her own authority and authenticity. How will you write toward the truth? How will you wade in, deep? How will you know what is superfluous and what matters? Where is the artist in you? What can you do to a sentence?

Put present time down.

Teach yourself the range of your own voice.

TENSE?

SQUIRREL gymnastics on the roof, laughter over a bowl of soup, the scratch and smell of ink. The memoir makers are working, photographs on their knees, their pens pausing midsentence.

Bring a photograph of yourself at a childhood or adolescent turning point: That is the assignment. Write the story in present tense. What can you see, smell, hear—at eight years old, with your brother nearby; at sixteen, with your grandmother cooking; at thirteen, with your father at an implacable distance? Present tense is instinct, spontaneity, life gulped in, the primal. The senses are ripe, but there is no absolute knowing, not yet in this trembling moment, of what will teach or linger.

> *It's my brother and me. The sun is glare and heat, and we're out walking.*

> *She's teaching me to cook—sharpening the blade, snapping the stems off the big-leafed parsley, and I am watching.*

> *We have come to the hard edge of the wide canyon, and the bugs are out. I'm angry.*

With the present-tense fragments set aside, the makers of memoir begin again, the same photos on their knees— the same people, the same action, the same fusing of flame to wick. But now past tense is the method. Now wisdom is the privilege. Now the urgency isn't simply about the details but about the process of bridging the distance.

> *I wasn't the brother I should have been.*

> *She died before I understood what it was she meant to teach me.*

> *I never asked him why he brought me there, what he thought that I might see.*

Past or present? Present or past? It's going to make a difference. Tense announces predilection and instinct. On the one hand: sense and detail, anecdote, in-your-face, it's happening, you're with me. On the other: cogitation, meditation, speculation, consideration, the sense of something measured. The heart and the mind. The eye and the *I*. It's still, in some fashion, alive, or it was. One or the other is going to appeal. One or the other will be right.

"Half my life ago," Darin Strauss begins his memoir, *Half a Life*, "I killed a girl." There's nothing but past tense for this, don't you agree? If you want proof, try writing the sentence in present tense. See how fast it falls apart. See what it does to the tone, the pretext, the moral authority of the author. Darin Strauss could not write his book in present tense. Not if he wanted our respect.

Gail Caldwell, too, had little choice in her memoir, *Let's Take the Long Way Home*, but to tell her story from the perspective of right now. She has been ruminating. She has been thinking. It's not the death of her best friend that she wants to posit as the headline. It's the struggle afterward to come to terms.

It's an old, old story: I had a friend and we shared everything, and then she died and so we shared that, too.

The year after she was gone, when I thought I had passed through the madness of early grief, I was on the path at the Cambridge reservoir where Caroline and I had walked the dogs for years. It was a winter afternoon and the place was empty—there was a bend in the road, with no one ahead of or behind me, and I felt a desolation so great that for a moment my knees wouldn't work. "What am I supposed to do here?" I asked her aloud, by now accustomed to conversations with a dead best friend. "Am I just supposed to keep going?" My life had made so much sense alongside hers: For years we had played the easy, daily game that intimate connection implies. One ball, two gloves, equal joy in the throw and the return. Now I was in the field without her: one glove, no game. Grief is what tells you who you are alone.

Could Loren Eiseley's *All the Strange Hours*, written late in life to examine a life, have any real meaning if it had been rendered in present tense? Wasn't he writing—and aren't we reading—so that we might know what age ultimately teaches?

It was a time of violence, a time of hate, a time of sharing, a time of hunger. It was all that every human generation believes it has encountered for the very first time in human history. Life is a journey and eventually a death. Mine was no different than those others. But this is in retrospect. At that time I merely lived, and each day, each night, was different.

Now look at what Mark Richard does with *House of Prayer No. 2*. Look at how he puts us right there, in the infinite strangeness of his childhood, where he is considered a "special child" with all that that phrase can connote, and where he gets sent (it's devastating) to fix that problem with his hips. It's just one of many wrenching, near-impossible scenes:

They wheel you down to the ward, and it's been cleft palate season. There are a lot of children running around with complicated black stitchery on their upper lips. Some look like little Hitlers, others look like black-whiskered cats. They put you on the big sunporch with some older black boys, and you're glad to find Michael Christian. Nurse Wilfong comes to see you and says how you've grown, must have been your mama's cooking, and you look toward the little sunporch and ask where Jerry is, and she holds your face in her hands and bends over and says, *Jerry died.*

Flip this to past tense—the same details, the same sad dying—and you have a different story. You have the need to explain more than one wants to have explained. You put knowing over feeling.

Two more pairings, now, for you to appraise. Both are the first paragraphs of their respective books. Both take their inspiration from memories of a childhood home. Both set into motion explorations of growing up in a "different" kind of world. Both are designed to bring the outsider in. But look at what tense does—which doors it opens and which it shuts.

There is laughter. There is the sharp report of a slamming door and the staccato of high heels crossing the ceramic tiles of the atrium garden. There is the reveille shout to the servants' quarters, the slap of sandals making their way to the animal pens, the *skrawk* of chickens as they are pulled from their cages, one by one, into the ink of night. It is three o'clock, before the light of day. —Marie Arana, *American Chica*

That our family's home was a school for the deaf did not seem in any way extraordinary to Reba, Andy, and me. Lexington School for the Deaf was simply where we came from. Our apartment was on the third floor of the southern wing of the building, above the nursery school and adjacent to the boys' dormitory. The walls and doors, incidental separations between our living space and the rest of the building, were routinely disregarded. Our father might be called away from the table in the middle of dinner; we children often played down the hall with the kids from the dorm. It wasn't until Reba, my older sister, proved at age six to be a sleepwalker—discovered one night riding the elevator in her pajamas—that our parents even thought to install a proper lock on the front door. —Leah Hager Cohen, *Train Go Sorry*

Marie Arana is telling her story in a vivid, emotive present tense. A slamming door. Staccato heels. Reveille shouts. Chicken *skrawk*. Leah Hager Cohen makes a different choice, writing, as she does, in a muted, more rational, more cerebral past tense. There are no sounds here, in this paragraph. No *skrawks*, no shouts. Hager lived, after all, among the deaf. It is neither her task nor her purpose to insert her readers inside the noisy, immediate bustle of childhood.

The transuding present tense, then? The phrenic past? Sometimes, but not always. Because certainly past-tense memoirs or memoiristic scenes can be and often are as vivid, as intense, as suspenseful as those written in the tense of *now*. No one, for example, has ever claimed that Jeannette Walls in *The Glass Castle* did not start out with a deeply visceral bang. Her past tense is electrifying, absorbing, frightening, and also essential here. It deepens our trust, reassures us, somehow, that these tales of a feral childhood have been sifted and sorted over time.

I was on fire.

It's my earliest memory. I was three years old, and we were living in a trailer park in a southern Arizona town whose name I never knew. I was standing on a chair in front of the stove, wearing a pink dress my grandmother had bought for me. Pink was my favorite color. The dress's skirt stuck out like a tutu, and I liked to spin around in front of the mirror, thinking I looked like a ballerina. But at that moment, I was wearing the dress to cook hot dogs, watching them swell and bob in the boiling water as the late-morning sunlight filtered in through the trailer's small kitchenette window.

Neither past tense nor present tense is generally wrong, then, nor generally right. And other tenses, too, can be and often are effectively deployed; future perfect is, for example, ripe with possibilities (*I will have learned; I will have lost; he will have left me, but I don't know that yet*). And sometimes—indeed, often—multiple tenses appear in a single memoir as authors wend back and forth through the years. Time is the memoirist's salvation and sin. Time is the tease and the puzzle. Time is the trickster, the tormentor, the vexer. Time solved or resolved is memoir mostly mastered.

Mary Karr brilliantly deploys dual tenses in her classic memoir, *The Liars' Club*. She even confides her strategy: "My father comes into focus for me on a Liars' Club afternoon. He sits at a wobbly card table weighed down by a bottle. Even now the scene seems so real to me that I can't but write it in the present tense."

In *Eat, Pray, Love*, Elizabeth Gilbert also makes fluid use of *it happened then, it's happening right now*. On a single page, in sections divided by white space, she addresses her readers with sentences like these: "I was with Luca the first time I ever tried eating the intestines of a newborn lamb,"

and "Sometimes I wonder what I'm doing here, I admit it."
She was and she is. It's okay. We're not confused.

But we your eager readers will only get it if you have
been deliberate and smart. Passage by passage, chapter by
chapter, you must decide how you will use tense to your
advantage. To constrain or to free. To mark yourself as a
certain *kind* of writer. To shape the story you wish to tell. To
put aspects of your story *at stake*.

FIND YOUR FORM

YOU noticed something back there, didn't you? It caught your eye. That Mark Richard fragment—that *you* instead of *I*. But aren't we talking about the single-letter pronoun when we're talking about memoir? Aren't we talking about ourselves? Why would Richard tell his story with a *you*? And come on, let's be honest, call a spade a spade: Is he even *allowed* to?

He does it because, in this case, the *you* is more intimate, more forgiving, more moving than the *I* ever will be. It enables Richard to say things about himself and his ungodly circumstance that would be otherwise unthinkable. Richard is, as we now know, a special child. There's something nearly ferocious about him, nearly feral, and besides, his legs don't work. His hips "click and pop." He is poor and from the South, and his father is wrecked by a cruel streak. We readers know what is coming. It helps if we can (just slightly) avert our eyes. Richard's second person allows us to do this. It gentles his story, yields something lush and kinder, less abrasive, and somehow (despite the many missing pieces) whole. Richard has done what he must do, first, to make his own story writable for himself and, second, to draw his readers near.

Are you still thinking that this is but a stylistic tic or trick? Have I failed to convince you? All right, then. Convince yourself. Take the passage that I quoted in the previous chapter and rewrite it in first person, as best you can. I asked my students to do this one semester. Here is what Beryl (who hit the assignment out of the park) wrote:

I made my way around the familiar ward. There were cleft palates everywhere, kids with black stitches all over their faces. Their faces used to make me cringe, but now they just made me giggle. For some, the stitches were concentrated in the center of the upper lip, just like Hitler's. Other stitches looked more like a cat's whiskers; thin black lines covering the outer edges. These stitches comforted me in a way, made me feel like I was home. As I made my way out onto the big sun porch, I scanned for familiar faces. A feeling of relief passed over me once I recognized Michael. Made me feel like I wasn't so much of a stranger, after all. When I saw Nurse Wilfong, a smile spread across her face. "My how you've grown!" She fussed and fussed, remarking on Mama's cooking and how big I had gotten and how much she had missed me. I had missed her too. As I continued to scan for familiar faces, I realized one was missing. "Where's Jerry?" A dark cloud passed over Nurse Wilfong's face. I knew what she was going to say before she even said it. A million thoughts passed through my mind—chess, the blue plastic plate, his legs. And as she uttered the words that I had predicted, I began to sob.

Decide for yourself. Which version of the story takes you deeper? Which puts you in the ward, with the heat, with the missing friend, with the despair? As Beryl reminds us by way of her alternative example, saying less is often more, indirection has its emotive appeal, and the overly self-assertive *I* can feel like an ambush. The second person, in *House of Prayer No. 2*, does not ask for empathy. It earns it.

bell hooks slides all across the grammatical spectrum to render *Bone Black*—deploying first person singular (*I*), first person plural (*we*), third person plural (*they*), and third person feminine singular (*she*) to quilt together her account of growing up readerly, passionate, different, and black in the South. In sixty-one abbreviated chapters—prose poems, really—hooks's pronouns are an endless source of suspense, a slowly depuzzled tension. "Mama has given me a quilt from her hope chest," the book begins, a false promise of the familiar.

But like Mark Richard, hooks soon finds the need to put some distance between her now self and her then self, and a switch to a new pronoun gives her that freedom: "She was considered a problem child, a child intent on getting her own way." Throughout the book, hooks will transition from the choral *we* to the lonely *I*, often within a fluid paragraph:

We learn about color with crayons. We learn to tell the difference between white and pink and a color they call Flesh. The flesh-colored crayon amuses us. Like white it never shows up on the thick Manila paper they give us to draw on, or on the brown paper sacks we draw on at home. Flesh we know has no relationship to our skin, for we are brown and brown and brown like all good things. And we know that pigs are not pink or white like these flesh people. We secretly love pigs, especially me. I like to watch them lie in the mud, covering themselves in the cool red mud that is like clay, that is flaming red hot like dirt on fire.

hooks's memoir, first published in 1996, is imagistic and suggestive, far more about what was gleaned and felt than about the contour of events. hooks has a plan; she has a method. She explains herself in the foreword:

Sometimes memories are presented in the third person, indirectly, just as all of us sometimes talk about things that way. We look back as if we are standing at a distance. Examining life retrospectively we are there and not there, watching and watched. Evoking the mood and sensibility of moments, this is an autobiography of perceptions and ideas. The events described are always less significant than the impressions they leave on the mind and heart.

I offer these examples (and of course there are others, notably Ned Zeman's brilliant *The Rules of the Tunnel*) with the hope that you, taking note, will feel liberated. Memoir, the *I* genre, need not box you in. Memoir calls for experimentation, leaps of faith, new takes on the old truth serums. Memoir writers should not automatically assume that the *I* will be sufficiently bold and bright for their stories.

Nor should they assume—should *you* assume—that words alone will be sufficient. Look at the ways that Orhan Pamuk uses photographs—historical photographs, family photographs, both art and documentary photographs—not just to illustrate his memoir, *Istanbul*, but also to generate a state of melancholy, a very particular mood. Or consider Dorothy Allison's use of family snapshots in *Two or Three Things I Know for Sure*. Even as she warns us that she may be embroidering her history and her people, even as her two or three learned things overwrite one another and multiply and ascend, Allison grounds us, with those photographs, in the immutable real—real people, real postures, real poses, real losses. Allison's photographs are her hard-core, tack-sure facts. They are among the reasons that we, despite her own disclaimers, trust her.

It's entirely possible, finally, that words and photographs, melded tenses and unexpected pronouns won't be enough, that you'll still be out there floundering for a way to tell the truth. Maybe the complexity of all you have to say— the overt stories, the hidden ones, the surfeit of details, the unspeakable pangs—can only be captured illustratively, comic-book style. Perhaps you—like Art Spiegelman, Harvey Pekar, Alison Bechdel, Marjane Satrapi, and others— have a gift for doing more with a pencil than simply scratching out the alphabet.

If that's the case, pull Bechdel's graphic memoir *Fun Home* off the shelf and study it for a very long time. Ask yourself what her illustrations do to deepen her story, to draw readers in, to re-create but not to persecute her terribly complicated father. How is an illustration different from a photograph? What degree of complexity is enabled by thought bubbles, gutters, captions, the signaled sound effect? What can a graphic memoir do, and what could you do with it?

Find your form. Work beyond the box. Secure a workable frame.

PHOTO SHOP

WRITING indulges the myth of continuity. Photographs suggest the significance of the single instant. Ever since a fourth-grade teacher helped me turn a musty Quaker Oats box into a pinhole camera, I've been chasing photographs. Since I fell hard for words (the sound of them, their shape) at about the same time, I've been caught, eternally thereafter, within the seductive snare of both.

That's not a bad thing.

In fact, I'm not entirely sure that I would still be writing today if I didn't have—or, more important, didn't *take*—photographs. So affixed an appendage is my Sony DSLR-A700 (I wear it loose, dangling from one shoulder; I wear it cradled in one hand; I wear it like a necklace on windy winter days) that I am known by some as the Crazy Lady. That camera-toting enthusiast.

But listen: The weight of the camera reminds me to see. It helps me decide against deciding that my world is overly familiar, already known. I look for cracks and fissures, for the new or newly announced. I look for water to run a different color in the stream, or for the sun to strike the pond in winter with delirious force. If I can't see, then I don't know, and if I don't know, I'm not writing, and while some may question the value of words, or of memoir in particular, I will again make this claim: Words rendered true spook and spur us. They expect *of* us. They expect *for* us. Photographs do the same thing: "Your photography is a record of your living, for anyone who really sees," said Paul Strand.

A little to the right, with a photograph, a little to the left, and everything changes. Zoom in, zoom out, and you have a new story. Consider what happens when you replace your wide-angle lens with a macro. Suddenly you go from the sweet blue bend of long horizons and bottom-bowled clouds to the bizarrely microscopic. Between rain bursts, you'll find me crouching in my garden with a macro, dialing in and out of temporal focus, catching the reflections off a puddled stamen, discovering the zebra stripes of an iris. I'll be thinking about how razor-edged the lily is, or how skirted and blurred the hydrangea seems, when photographed from above. I brace myself for the macro lens. I try not to breathe. I snap.

"I prowled the streets all day, feeling very strung-up and ready to pounce, determined to 'trap' life—to preserve life in the act of living. Above all, I craved to seize, in the confines of one single photograph, the whole essence of some situation that was in the process of unrolling itself before my eyes." The words of Henri Cartier-Bresson.

"To quote out of context is the essence of the photographer's craft. His central problem is a simple one: what shall he include, what shall he reject? The line of decision between in and out is the picture's edge. While the draughtsman starts with the middle of the sheet, the photographer starts with the frame." The words of John Szarkowski.

I ask my students to bring their cameras to class. I ask them to go out and snatch up ten pictures. *Photograph what interests you,* I say. *And come back in a half hour.* And then I wait. Okay, I don't actually just sit there and wait. I go out with my own camera, photographing students taking photographs. Crazy Lady and whatnot.

Out of breath, trailing laughter, already scheming about the words they will put down for the assignment they are sure they will be given, the students return. Easy peasy, right? The Crazy Lady wants them to find the words to describe the best-slash-favorite-slash-most-iconic-slash-killer-interesting picture(s) taken? Nope. Too obvious. Too surface. The assignment I give goes something like this: Study the background of any chosen photograph. Not the foreground, the background. What's in the picture that you didn't see when you were snapping? What lies beyond the chosen subject—just to the right or to the left? How do the borderlands shadow and shape the subject? What does the startle of the once-unnoticed detail suggest to you? What would happen if this small thing—and not the obvious thing, the central thing, the thing easily seized and snatched—was the start of your story?

Look deeper.

See smarter.

Consider.

So that the plate of cookies I had brought to class and was photographed as a student's tenth subject is suddenly perceived as the wooden table beneath the plate—scarred and secretive. Or the photograph of the man on the bike is not a photograph of a man on a bike after all but instead an image of the pane of glass behind him, a peek inside an urban gym and the endless going-nowhere of treadmill athletes; the bike moves, the treadmill athletes do not, tell me the story. Or maybe the streetscape snapped in a windy hurry is actually a portrait of a traffic light, frozen red: *Stop. Now.* Or maybe that portrait of the campus compass tiled into Locust Walk is not a portrait of a compass after all but of a chicken, off in the distance—or, as Liz wrote, "a man in a chicken *costume.* Slight difference. My eyes trace up his body from the large orange feet, past the heinous yellow feathers, up to the face of a brunette boy with a backwards baseball cap. I smile to myself. *This is Penn,* I think, *utterly ridiculous and entirely beautiful at the same time.*"

Too many people think when they are thinking (theoretically) about the memoir they feel bound to write that they know what the story is. "My memoir is about what happened to me," they will say, and then recount, in a sentence or two, the headline news. A child lost. An illness overcome. A wicked mother. A farm recovered. A month in Africa. A liar! A cheat! A scandal survived!

But the headlines are only the headlines, a blare. Or, as Vivian Gornick writes in *The Situation and the Story,* they are merely situation. What readers want is meaning. They want a story so rich, complex, thought through, and learned from that it can't, in fact, be revealed by a headline or two; it can't be satisfactorily summarized. Readers want to be able to participate. They want to discover, with the writer, those images at the edge of the frame, or over to the side, or just a tad blurred that have, as it turns out, something rich to say. Something powerful and universal. Something extracted and framed as, in the words of Loren Eiseley in *All the Strange Hours,* "the unique possession of a single life":

There are pictures that hang askew, pictures with outlines barely chalked in, pictures torn, pictures the artist has striven unsuccessfully to erase, pictures that only emerge and glow in a certain light. They have all been teleported, stolen, as it were, out of time. They represent no longer the sequential flow of ordinary memory. They can be pulled about on easels, examined within the mind itself. The act is not one of total recall like that of the professional mnemonist. Rather it is the use of things extracted from their context in such a way that they have become the unique possession of a single life.

Yours is a single life. It is *the* single life of your memoir.

DO YOU LOVE?

IN his letters to the nineteen-year-old Franz Xaver Kappus, Rainer Maria Rilke said this about love:

> It is also good to love: because love is difficult. For one human being to love another human being: that is perhaps the most difficult task that has been entrusted to us, the ultimate task, the final test and proof, the work for which all other work is merely preparation. That is why young people, who are beginners in everything, are not yet capable of love: it is something they must learn. With their whole being, with all their forces, gathered around their solitary, anxious, upward-beating hearts, they must learn to love.

Not long ago, I read these words to a classroom full of eighth-grade girls. *True or false?* I asked. Some heads shaking no. Some heads shaking yes. Then I made a request: *Write for five minutes about one thing that you are learning to love.*

Anything? one freckle-faced girl asked, after everyone else had started scribbling.

Anything, I said.

She scrunched her nose. She scratched her head. She couldn't get a toehold. I told her a little about me, about how I've lived wanting, reaching, exuding, falling, again reaching and again wanting more. I loved the wild, reckless freedom of the ice, I said, explaining my youthful figure skating years. I loved watching two pools of watercolors merge and make a brand-new color. I loved my cat, a calico I'd rescued from a graveyard. I loved the fancy things that a guy named F. Scott Fitzgerald could do with words.

But still the girl pondered as other pencils scratched, and so I read her a poem about applesauce by Ted Kooser. It's not a poem about love, exactly. But it is about its cousin, like about what apples do when boiling on a stove, about how a kitchen changes when suffused by the smell of warm apples.

Oh, the girl said. I don't like applesauce, she said. But I do like sunny afternoons when I'm homework-free, I like talking to friends on my pink iPhone, I like the ring I wear on my pinkie and (possibly) the person who gave me the ring. She smiled. She got to work. A fragment of a poem by the former poet laureate had given this still-learning adolescent a place to start. It had set her moving in the direction of love.

Do you love? Are you still learning to love? How hard is this love thing, for you? It's not a question reserved for the young. It's a question for all of us, and it's a question we must repeatedly ask ourselves, especially when we're writing memoir. If we don't know what we love—if we're not yet capable of it; if we're stuck in a stingy, fisted-up place; if we're still too angry to name the color of the sun—it is probably too soon to start the sorting and stacking and shaping that is memoir. Maybe we haven't learned enough yet. Maybe we haven't sufficiently tempered our disappointment with grace. Maybe we haven't stopped hurting long enough to look up and see the others who hurt with us, who stand in our (it only seems invisible) community. Maybe we only have words right now for our mighty wounds and our percolating scars. And if that's the case, let's step aside, for those words alone are the stuff of litanies, screeds, judgments, and declamations; they're the stuff of long and lonely writing rides. You'll be looking at you, talking through you, talking about you, talking at me, and it'll all be bump and grind.

Call me sentimental; others have. Remind me that the world is dark and ugly, that people are cruel, that injustice reigns, that children suffer, that the wrong people win, the wrong people triumph. I know. I have been there. I have seen. I have lost to the infidels once or twice myself, and that woman—that woman with the short auburn hair and the bright red lipstick who laughed at how I danced and moved and talked, who called me *old*—she had *no* business making me feel like that, doubt like that, stop sleeping. Seriously, she didn't. But no memoir is worth reading if it is not leavened with beauty and love. And no memoirist should start her work until she can, with authority, write about the things she loves.

So think about it. Put yourself in that half place between dream and story, and hover. Think about how the world leaks and scrambles out toward possibilities and how, between divisions, under stones, in the eyes of a child, in the spark of first sun on a river reflecting blue, passions get their running start—or should. Think about the smallest things that make you happy—Kooser's apples, maybe, or the backyard oak, or a full moon rising on a high tide, or your mother, after all, or the man you're actually glad you married, or the child you thought you'd never have, or the neighbor you so purposely ignored until his pear trees bloomed such a snow-fantastic white. Sit in a chair and conjure beauty and goodness, the stepping-stones of love. Make a list. Tangle up with metaphor. Practice gratitude. Rest assured you'll be given a chance to tell the *whole* story soon. But start, for now, with love.

By the way: If anyone calls you sentimental while you sit there locking language to love, remind him that love is the hardest thing we do, the most complicated, riddled, as it is, with guilt and forgiveness, anxiety and insecurity, our supremely human need for redemption. Tell him that hate, anger, retribution, and clenched jaws are going-nowhere stories, unidirectional shouts. Tell him that love is where life stories start, no matter what one is writing about.

Maybe he'll remember the things he loves, too.

Maybe helping him remember is one of the many things that your memoir, when you write your memoir, can and must ultimately do. "Love, like light," Adam Gopnik said, "is a thing that is enacted better than defined: we know it afterward by the traces it leaves on paper."

WHETHER THE WEATHER

I know what the weather was when I entered my husband's dorm room at Yale University to say, *Yes. Okay. I will marry you.* It was February's version of cold, and lonely birds squawked outside, and though it was late afternoon, the air was the color of morning fog. I had taken the train up, found my way to his room. I had had all those hours to decide whether this artist from El Salvador whose paintings I knew better than his ambitions, whose family I had never met, who favored the black and blue of night over my own peach-tinted dawn was, as they say, The One. I was twenty-three. I felt, at that time, old. I watched the weather through the scratched window of the Amtrak train and tried to read the signs in the air, translate the frantic cautions of the tossed and hieratic birds.

I know what the weather was when my mother died. I had spent the final difficult months at her side, had sung her songs, had placed and replaced the flowers and photographs, the potted lemon tree, the Bible in what would be her last room; I had heard (will never forget hearing) what she meant for me to hear. I had said good-bye because I knew it was her time, because I had somehow understood that she wished her dying to be a private thing, and so I was out, walking in the dark beneath a few bright stars when I felt the nudge of a breeze on one shoulder. A knock. And then a whoosh. "Mom," I said, for it was her, I knew. Her final earthly touch.

I know what the weather was on the night before we drove our son back to his second semester of college. We'd waited all day for the snow, and when it came the flakes were saucers—huge and slant, conjoined. We had had our time as a family of three, but the next day our boy would be headed back to the hills, to Literature and Advertising, to Probability and World Cultures, to a sound engineering booth and a dorm. So we drove through the night on backcountry roads—the snow falling, the moon rising, the world bright and wholly bittersweet, for what does one do with the deep, rutted, impossible love for children who grow, too, who emerge, like us, into the age they are becoming? What does one do but drive across roads and inside the shell of a heart-quelled silence, anticipating tomorrow? For that is what the weather was that night—a heart-quelled silence.

I remember weather. Do you? I am *convinced* by it, so on mornings when I wake to the whisper-rush of snow, when I feel the roof heavying down, the silence deeper than the previous night, my sentences grow long, embedded, rounded. But then, on days that are blue sky and angling for warmth, my sentences take on the connotations of jive. They're all quick steps and electric slide. There is no escaping this, or there shouldn't be. Weather, and how we both live and write it, must enter—should enter—into the memories we make and resurrect.

Look outside, go outside, write this right now: The quality of breeze. The evidence of dew. The pile of clouds on the horizon. Find the words. It doesn't matter how tired you are. It doesn't matter if you think there's nothing new here, if weather has been done before, if weather isn't (to you, at least) the story. An alive sky is a whole soul; you must let it filter through you. Watermelon. Lilac. Gunmetal. Blue. Upticking fog. Rain as the sound. Sun as a caution sign. A moon that has gone fishing. A cranberry-colored landscape. Cold for August. Thunder like a jet just off the tarmac, hail the size of rock salt, the straight white nails of rain driving through, or just the gray pale pink before a storm, or, again, fog curl with a mind of its own.

Write the weather of this instance; find the words. Put yourself in a weather zone, and then let your mind drift back. Write the weather of your wedding day, now, or the weather of your first school day, or the weather of a funeral day, or the weather of a carefree day. What is on your page? Is it rhapsodic? Is it stark? Is it original? Is it true? Where do weather memories and weather words take you?

Too many people forget, when writing memoir, the power of context, the evocative tug of the broader tapestry. They'll focus on lines of action—on he said/she said/they did. They'll show you the crimes or craft a five-page monologue or slam you with the simmering gossip—*I was young; I lost my mind*. And in all this rendering of the facts as best as any facts can be recalled and subsequently rendered, the wider world gets lost, the extenuating circumstances, the reality that things are always bigger than you or me.

Don't lose the wider world. Carry more than the events themselves forward. Carry the images, the sensory shocks, the small interludes of cloud play, sun scream, the smell of rain, the yaw of an old birch branch, the scattering of sky.

It's possible—even probable—that there will be a lesson in all of this, that background will again become foreground, that what appeared to be inconsequential at the time was in fact a foreshadowing or a judgment. Pay attention to weather. Bend it into words. Ask yourself if it has a rightful place in the memoir you will be writing. "The range of a writer's metaphor is a measure of the range of his cognition," Leon Wieseltier once wrote, in a review of *Saul Bellow: Letters*. I am going to borrow that line and make a few substitutions: The range of a writer's weather vocabulary is a measure of the range of her perception.

I'll close this weather exhortation (rant?) with this: I have a friend named Alyson Hagy. We met years ago, thanks to a grant we'd both won, and she has gone on to do so many important things as both an author of stunning talent and a brilliant teacher at the University of Wyoming in Laramie. I learn important things from Alyson—about teaching, about writing, about the power of humility—and because she lives so many miles from where I do, our conversation is almost exclusively over e-mail. Nearly a thousand e-mails from Alyson now, and almost every one of them relates something of her weather. The early snows. The late thaws. The confusion of fish in hoary streams. The windy disruption of bird life.

"The hint of autumn was subtle," Alyson has written. "The way the clouds built in the morning—not as mountains of cumulonimbus but as layers of cumulus and cirrus. The early cry of the fledgling red-tailed hawks that have nested in the neighborhood and are now just out on their

own—so wary, yet so dangerous (they have quieted the local crows). The way the dust on the breeze smelled cool instead of hot. It's usually 50 in the morning now instead of 55.
The days are still glorious and bright, but you can see how
the robins are hustling to plump up for departure."

There's story there, the tantalizing breath of memoir.
There's Alyson yielding the wide, ungovernable world of
her weather and—at the same time—her way of seeing, her
patterns of perception. Tell me how you see your weather,
and you will tell me something of yourself. I want to know
not just *what* you see but also *how* you see, in every line that
you call memoir.

LANDSCAPE IT

ON the day that I turned forty-one I found myself at a pleasure garden some ten minutes down the road from where I live. I had gone alone. I was there just to be. I had written four books—four memoirs—and I was all done, I thought, with words. Sick of my own stories. Sick of my own responsibilities. Sick and tired and needing a world far more interesting, complex, mysterious, forgiving than I thought myself to be. You can worry yourself out as a writer. You can grow empty, redundant, spiritually thin. I had worried myself down to the bones.

Over the next two years I would visit that garden weekly during its open season. I would revel in all that I did not know, take small half steps toward knowledge. Gardeners would teach me. The weather would abrade me. The landscape would change the way I walked and saw. An old lady would ask me a question—*How do you see everything?*—and I would wonder my way toward an answer for days afterward. It was as if someone had taken a saw to my chest, split my rib cage, and made more room for my heart.

All throughout our lives, we move through, we move against, we move toward landscape. We dress for landscape.

We sweat the hills. We take our children to the ocean's edge. We rise at three in the morning to see how a certain rock face will hold the moon. We nestle close to the spray of a violent waterfall. We roll down the hill just past the forest. We gather the wildflowers because we can't take the rocky path home. We hurry our friends along, or we sneak out alone. We are shaped by landscape, and we tug at, plow into, level it ourselves, exerting our own ideas upon it.

> I conceived of the garden as a poem in stanzas. Each terrace contributes to the garden as a whole in the same way each stanza in a poem has a life of its own, and yet is part of a progressive whole as well.
>
> The form provides some degree of repose, letting our mind rest in the comparatively manageable unit of the stanza, or terrace. Yet there is also a need to move on, to look beyond the stanza, into the poem as a whole. —Stanley Kunitz, *The Wild Braid: A Poet Reflects on a Century in the Garden*

The beauty of a broken fountain, an old ramshackle mansion, a ruined hundred-year-old gasworks, the crumbling wall of an old mosque, the vines and plane trees intertwining to shade the old blackened walls of a wooden house—these are accidental. But when I visited the city's backstreets as a child, these painterly tableaux were so numerous it was difficult, after a point, to see them as unintended: these sad (now vanished) ruins that gave Istanbul its soul. But to "discover" the city's soul in its ruins, to see these ruins as expressing the

city's essence, you must travel down a long laby-
rinthine path strewn with historical accidents.
—Orhan Pamuk, *Istanbul*

It is interesting, given all the seething power of both the
rising and the ruined, how rarely landscape seeps convincingly into the work of aspiring memoirists. A country might
be named, or a mountain peak, or a flower. But by and large,
beginning memoirists tend to discard or forget to see the
power of earth vents and lava flows, caldera and geysers, the
frozen life inside the fossil, gorges and stalactite caves, ice
margins and deltas, skyscrapers and central parks. They con-
sign landscape to background, or render it as mere decora-
tion. They say, *I was here, here, here, and here*, but they do not
plumb here's depths.

No doubt some of my students would if the pieces we
work on weren't constrained by a certain word count.
Some of them would ultimately *get around* to landscape, but
getting around to landscape is not the same thing as deliberately mining it for metaphors and wisdoms, contours and
sensibilities. Getting around to landscape does not honor
landscape. It does not even begin to tap the possibilities
that range within.

You don't need a geologist's vocabulary to write landscape. You don't need to go all textbook—kettle lake, oxbow
lake, fault spring, graben lake. In the right circumstances,
that kind of talk can take you and the reader somewhere.
But landscape simply drawn tells stories, too.

Consider this passage by Debra Marquart in *The Horizontal World*. The author is returning home, to her father's
funeral. She's revisiting familiar childhood terrain and seeing, in that patch of horizon, a magnetizing mythology.

On the morning of my father's funeral, as we came over the next rise, I saw we had three miles to go. This is Logan County. While it may be just another patch of flat horizon to someone driving through, to the people of my family it's the navel of the earth, the place from which all things flow and to which all things return in time.

For Susan Brind Morrow in *The Names of Things*, time spent observing the natural world leads to quiet reconciliation and deep insights. The first paragraph excerpted below is, absolutely, pure description. But it isn't long before these crabs, this white sand, those mangroves are yielding an understanding of language itself.

As I walk along the shore of the Red Sea at dawn a hundred pale pink crabs scuttle carefully back across and into the white sand. Behind a sharp crust of coral a rock crab, seaweed-green edged with red, pries the back off of a sand crab and feeds. It is not so easily frightened and merely watches me. There are tiny porcelain-blue crabs in the mangroves a few miles south, popping out of the dense muddy quicksand like living jewels.

In this harsh environment, life itself is a gorgeous miracle, coming out of the barren desert, out of the bitter sea: hals, the sea of salt. . . .

Words begin as description. They are prismatic, vehicles of hidden, deeper shades of thought. You can hold them up at different angles until the light bursts through in an unexpected color. The word carries the living thing concealed across millennia.

In her classic memoir, *Refuge*, Terry Tempest Williams takes us into a world of enormous beauty and troubling wreckage. Williams's mother is dying of ovarian cancer. A bird refuge is being threatened. Williams is losing the things she values most and struggling to come to terms with her grief. Here the natural world does not merely suggest metaphors, or offer escape, or divulge some previously foggy truth. Here Williams *becomes* landscape. Landscape steadies her.

> I know the solitude my mother speaks of. It is what sustains me and protects me from my mind. It renders me fully present. I am desert. I am mountains. I am Great Salt Lake. There are other languages being spoken by wind, water, and wings. There are other lives to consider: avocets, stilts, and stones. Peace is the perspective found in patterns. When I see ring-billed gulls picking on the flesh of decaying carp, I am less afraid of death. We are no more and no less than the life that surrounds us. My fears surface in my isolation. My serenity surfaces in my solitude.

There are writers, like Rick Bragg, who give us landscape first, as here in the opening scene of *All Over but the Shoutin'*.

> My mother and father were born in the most beautiful place on earth, in the foothills of the Appalachians along the Alabama-Georgia line. It was a place where gray mists hid the tops of low, deep-green mountains, where redbone and bluetick hounds flashed through the pines as they chased

possums into the sacks of old men in frayed overalls, where old women in bonnets dipped Bruton snuff and hummed "Faded Love and Winter Roses" as they shelled purple hulls, canned peaches and made biscuits too good for this world.

There are writers, like Isabel Allende, in *My Invented Country*, who take us south, into the sun.

I recall that my family and I, loaded with bundles, climbed onto a train that traveled at a turtle's pace through the inclement Atacama Desert toward Bolivia. Sun, baked rocks, kilometers and kilometers of ghostly solitudes, from time to time an abandoned cemetery, ruined buildings of adobe and wood. It was a dry heat where not even flies survived. Thirst was unquenchable. We drank water by the gallon, sucked oranges, and had a hard time defending ourselves from the dust, which crept into every cranny. Our lips were so chapped they bled, our ears hurt, we were dehydrated.

There are those—Mary Morris, *Nothing to Declare*—who will take us, so persuasively, to San Miguel that I later followed in her footsteps.

You come to the old Mexico, a lawless land. It is a landscape that could be ruled by bandits or serve as a backdrop for the classic Westerns, where all you expect the Mexicans to say is "*hombre*" and "*amigo*" and "*sí, señor.*" It is a land with colors. Desert colors.

Sand and sienna, red clay and cactus green, scattered yellow flowers. The sky runs all the ranges of purple and scarlet and orange. You can see dust storms or rain moving toward you. Rainbows are frequent. The solitude is dramatic.

There are those—read Mary Karr's *The Liars' Club*—who render the poison and slick of an oil refinery into some otherworldly landscape.

In the fields of gator grass, you could see the ghostly outline of oil rigs bucking in slow motion. They always reminded me of rodeo riders, or of some huge servant creatures rising up and bowing down to nothing in particular. In the distance, giant towers rose from each refinery, with flames that turned every night's sky an odd, acid-green color. The first time I saw a glow-in-the-dark rosary, it reminded me of those five-story torches that circled the town at night. Then there were the white oil-storage tanks, miles of them, like the abandoned eggs of some terrible prehistoric insect.

But you don't have to go south or into the purging desert or the sand and sienna of San Miguel to have something to say about landscape. You don't even have to walk a garden for two years, or attempt to build one, or find ghostly beauty within noxious fumes. Because landscape can be the tadpole creek that ran behind your neighbors' houses. It can be the field where you found your first fleck of shiny mica. It can be the curvy path between the trees that you ran that day, alone (again), frightened (terrified) after a teacher had taken you aside to say, *Your mother's been in a bad accident.*

Landscape can be your own backyard, or the unlanterned street with the single lit window of a hunched house. It can be big trees or skimpy trees, the rocks where the bobcats prowl or the golden fields of wheat historied by the old grain silo where the black crows make their home. It can be the milky blue fence of the horse show grounds or the round-bellied towers of a strange skyline or the planted rectangles of mobile homes in a concentric trailer park. It can be ruins. Have you, now contemplating memoir, contemplated ruins? Do you know what you are missing? Let Christopher Woodward tell you: "When we contemplate ruins, we contemplate our own future."

Stop reading this book; put it down. Pick up a pen and write what you can see from the nearest window—those fixed forms of your world. Not the weather; that's transient. Not the people; they'll come and go. Look for the bulwarks, the hollows, the cracks, the rounded masses, the chiseled, the pillared, the rising, the sunk, the missing. Geometry should factor in. Palettes and hues. Shades and pockmarks. Rough and smooth. Deliberate and accidental. Verging on gone. Write it all down so that when you send it to me or share it with your neighbor or blog it for the world, we can *see.*

Now close your eyes and find within yourself a landscape from long ago. Put this down, too, best as you can. Don't pretend to see what you cannot. Don't airbrush this exercise for the sake of faux completeness. Just put down what your memory gives you, as fragile or flimsy as that seems. Then ask yourself questions like these: Why *this* landscape? Why its incompleteness? Why have you focused on the upright shafts and not on all of that which blunders horizontal? Why don't the colors come back, or if they do, why are they so loud and self-insistent? To what part of yourself, or your story, does this landscape return you?

And what do you know now that you couldn't have known then?

Where does landscape take you?

THINK SONG

THE notebook in which I write these words is slick and sloganed: *I am fairly certain that, given a Cape and a nice tiara, I could save the world.* That's the front cover. Inside, two words and a period (I take special note of the period): *write love.*

It would be impossible not to when writing of my students. It would be impossible not to *feel.* Because look at them—their heads bowed to the prayer of a memory teased forward by the music of Astor Piazzolla. They write to the tango, to the slow andante that spins in the old computer's tray and sifts through dusty speakers. They walk themselves back, their eyes half-closed, in a room crowded with tossed coats and fatigued bags, the Styrofoam crypt of abandoned French fries, the molder of snow that has collected in the treads of their boots.

It has been the winter of white skies and frozen slicks, but here they are, in a room of andante, shoulder to shoulder, remembering other temperatures, a different face of the sun, because that is what I have asked for here. Ten minutes spent remembering a childhood encounter with weather—a moment evoked by the Piazzolla song.

Watching them remember, I remember, too. The fog curl and cliff erosion of San Francisco. Lagoons drenched with dawn pink. The chill in the underskirt of an ocean current. The smell of Spanish moss after a torrent of afternoon rain. The split of a lightning-fractured sky. I watch, and as I watch, on torn pages and laptop screens, a storm breaks and clouds gather and elsewhere there is sun.

One sentence, or two. Bold. Unpredictable. True. Read aloud from what you've just written, I say, and the students do—and in their work I hear the dawning of new voices, new sounds, lines aided by song. "We will go where the wind takes us," Dascher writes, a beginning. Often the students are surprised by the sentences they produce. They didn't, they tell me, know they were capable of this—these collisions, these rhythms, these isolated or meshed or intravenous details. Something is happening. Something is new. Hold on, go further, see what you're capable of.

A small moment. A beat of silence. And now I trade the Piazzolla song for the Benedictine monks of Santo Domingo de Silos. I ask the students, again, to sit and listen, dream backward, reinvent. Another day of weather. Another month, another year. Where does the music take them? What language enwraps that then most fully? Devotion and lift. Ease and inner stillness. Anticipation, too. What do you hear? I ask. Where are you? Write it. Let your words uncover you. Let your words *prove* you.

Across the campus, in darkened auditoriums, faculty pontificate, students take notes, and the business of actual learning goes on. But here in our room the monks are chanting and my students are sighing, tentative, wondering. They are going back in time, breaking the mold of the familiar in search of something equally true.

Maybe it doesn't sound all that Ivy League or résumé building to ask students to honor the smear of childhood or to heed the rhythms of remembered weather. Maybe I'm the only writing teacher spinning discs on ancient machines. And maybe it's a tad shy of rigorous to conduct a classroom full of eased-back kids—dreamers and window watchers, scribblers and flippers of pens, dismantlers of paper clips.

Maybe.

But I think not.

Because something always happens when I let foreign music spin. Shoulders drop. Postures settle. Words come out newly. Within the raw yelps of these music-infused exercises we discover, together, what the aspiring makers of memoir have within themselves to do, and to be. They haven't started writing true memoir yet. They haven't chosen a topic, delivered their proposals, made an explicit promise about form and meaning. All of that will come.

For now they are on speaking terms with a broader range of linguistic possibilities, and I'm going to keep them here for a while longer. There is still some not-yet-writing-memoir work to be done.

THE COLOR OF LIFE

HOURS before the forty-ninth National Book Awards ceremony got under way, Alane Salierno Mason, the editor who had found my first memoir in a slush pile and called me on my birthday to offer me a contract, remembered a room I had to see; we went. A lion, an edifice, a swoop of stairs, and then there it was: big as a city block and skied with permanent weather. There were six-hundred-pound tables and a constellation of polished lamps, people enough for a subway station, though this was the New York Public Library, the newly splendored Rose Main Reading Room. I thought I heard a holy hush. I felt drawn out, thrown out of kilter by the hundreds hunkered down with books.

A while later, John Updike took the stage at the Marriott Marquis to accept the 1998 award for Distinguished Contribution to American Letters. His voice had a quiet, avuncular appeal, and in that darkened room he stepped his audience back into the library of his youth, the glamour of a typeface, the beauty of a book "in proportion to the human hand." There were stacks of books on every table, images of books hung like pendants on the walls. There were authors in the room, editors, publishers, agents, reviewers; there were readers, and we understood why we had come.

The media, the next day and for days to come, would write of dark horses, battlefields, upset victories, dueling styles. They would tally winners and losers as if the making of books were a gamble or a sport. They would declaim the event because their heroes had not been crowned, because somehow they had not deduced the final outcome. But what too many lost in their rush for the headline was the reality of what the National Book Awards is meant to be: a celebration of books. A communion of stories. A tribute to the humanity of words.

When I think back on the utterly unforeseen honor of being named a National Book Award finalist, I remember the bewilderment at having been noticed for such a personal book about love and courage and the distilled sheen of hours spent with family and friends. But from the haze also rises the unforgettable voice of Gerald Stern, a poet who had been nominated that year for his collection *This Time: New and Selected Poems*. Something happened inside my head as Stern read his work out loud over the course of that two-day event—and that same thing still happens, all these years later, whenever I return to his lines on the page. Gerald Stern's poetry cures my migraines. It corrects my blood pressure and shakes me clean and clear; it cracks whatever veneer has settled in for whatever reasons veneers always do settle in.

Which is precisely what I want for my students, for all writers of memoir. No posturing. No attitude. No working off history. No easy riding. No simple chapter two. Because it doesn't matter how many essays you've already written, or how many books. It doesn't matter what others have said or what the juries have decided. It doesn't matter if you're sitting in an Ivy League classroom or at home alone. If you are not awake to the world, if you do not approach the work as if it is the first thing you've ever written or the last words you'll ever say, you have no business writing. Writing is not a task; it is no job. Writing is a privilege.

I use a Gerald Stern poem called "Eggshell" to help my students rid themselves of predictable responses, merely passable language, B-plus muddle. I read from the poem's start:

> The color of life is an almost pale white robin's green
> that once was bluer when it was in the nest,
> before the jay deranged the straw and warm flesh
> was in the shell. . . .

That's what I read—the first sentence of an impeccable poem—and then I stop, hold the silence, read again. "What is the color of life?" I ask, and before anyone has had a chance to answer, I insist that they write it down instead. *Their* color of life. *Their* hues. The economics of *their* relationships to things.

Tell me your color of life, and I will tell you who you are. But that isn't the point, not really. The point is for you to know who you are. The point is, once again, to stretch language. Here Nabil gives us red and blue and color reflected in faces. He gives us his colors. He gives us his soul.

> The branches on the tree above me spread their
> hands and fingers outward, obscuring the sun from
> my eyes but giving me a first-class view of the

brilliant blue sky beyond. A striking red cardinal fluttered in the breeze, and took off across my field of vision. Its movements and decisions are not random; they are calculated, deliberate, purposeful. The bird I saw had come from somewhere and was making its way to a place it decided it wanted to go. Each leaf of the tree, too, had seen things nothing else has ever seen, held secrets, experienced and lived the way nobody ever has before. The bird and the tree had stories worth knowing—stories that defined them, that nobody else could lay claim to. Life is the color reflected on people's faces as I walk by—a color that comes from within them, one that is shaped by their past and future. If we do not recognize our circumstances and our stories and hold them dear, then what do we have to recognize at all?

I HEAR VOICES

A fellow memoirist and reviewer writes: "I'm reading a memoir now where the author has written four chapters full of dialogue for events that occurred when she was four years old. Over half the book occurs before she is ten and it's all about what people said and felt. I don't see how much of this could possibly be true."

My friend's got this right: Nothing makes a reader question memoir more indignantly than the things set aside by quotation marks. You remember that whole entire feminist monologue that your mother delivered when she found you (at age three) smeared with her lipstick, wearing her stilettos? Were you taking dialogue notes twenty years ago when your husband decided to leave you for the cyclist he met at his dance class? You knew the word *testosterone* when you were five? You knew what *punk* meant? You were capable of irony? You recollect, in long-paragraph format, the words your mother said upon the death of your (young) childhood pet?

"Why is so much lost?" Joyce Carol Oates asks in her memoir *A Widow's Story*. "Our aural memories are weak, unreliable. We have all heard friends repeating fragments of conversations inaccurately—yet emphatically; not only language is lost but the tone, the emphasis, the *meaning*."

Unless you walked around your entire life with a tape recorder in your pocket, dialogue will become one of the greatest moral and storytelling conundrums you will face when writing memoir. You may feel that you need some of it, a smattering at least, to round out characters, change the pace, dissect the rub between what was thought and what was actually said. You may need dialogue because, in life, people talk to one another and readers want to know what they said; they want to know the *sound* of the relationships.

Dialogue isn't, strictly speaking, absolutely necessary in memoir. There's not a single chain of the stuff in all of *Bone Black*, the bell hooks memoir, for example. She doesn't need it because the anecdotal is not her concern; because her chapters are short; because the book, with all its invention and complexity, is never in need of a reprieve. Lucy Grealy and Elizabeth McCracken don't rely on dialogue to tell their remarkable stories (*Autobiography of a Face* and *An Exact Replica of a Figment of my Imagination*); it appears, but only rarely. Other memoirists—most, in fact—can't go the distance without a she-said.

When it is done right, it feels essential; it seems to bring us closer to the story's heart. Consider the exchange that sits toward the end of Mark Doty's *Heaven's Coast*. Wally, Doty's lover, is deep into his journey with AIDS. Concessions must be made, but Wally's reluctant. We don't need a lot of dialogue to understand how much this hurts not just Doty, the story's teller, but also Wally, its subject. We don't even need quotation marks. But we do need to know some of what's been said.

> The next morning, his anger is strenuous, and he's more passionate with refusal than I've seen him in months; this will *not* do.
>> I say, let's give it a try.
>> He says, No, I won't have it, no.
>> Just for a week?
>> Silence.
>> Let's see if we can't make it better, and then in a week, if you still don't like it, back it goes.

Similarly, this exchange from Terry Tempest Williams's *Refuge*. The quoted words are essential, I find, to helping the reader understand just how a dying mother and a grieving daughter are coming to their very different, respective terms.

> "What I have learned through all this," Mother says, "is that you just pick yourself up and go on."
> I rub her back while she talks.
>> "I have fought for so long and I have worked so hard to live through this summer, this fall, Christmas—and every minute has been worth it. And now, it feels good to give in. I am ready to go."
>> "Terry, you have accepted this, haven't you?"
>> "My soul has—but my mind has not."

Still, the act of writing dialogue for memoir feels just slightly akin to pinning the once-effervescent dragonfly to the black velvet backing in science class. You've got to be precise. You've got to spread the wings just right. You've got to protect those delicate saucer eyes, even if your hands are a tad sweaty and clumsy. You don't want to make it up, and you might not want to leave it out. Somebody help us with this.

Diaries and journals can be a boon. Transcripts are a blessing. Those who knowingly enter into an experience with the intention of writing memoir (a process known, among other names, as immersion memoir) can choose, and sometimes do choose, to bring a digital memory along. That was Buzz Bissinger's method as he wrote *Father's Day*. He took a trip. He brought his son. He recorded their conversations. Even so, Bissinger does not enclose his conversational threads inside quotation marks:

—Have you ever fallen in love with anybody?
—No.
—Have you ever had a girlfriend really?
—I think I like Shanna.
—Do you know what sex is?
—I've heard about it before.
—What is it?
—When you sleep together.
—Have you ever slept with anybody?
—No.
—Do you want to?
—No.
—Have you ever kissed anybody?
—No.

Somebody yells "Happy Birthday." The television screens show a catastrophic bridge collapse in Minneapolis. Nobody stops to watch.

—Do you hate it when I ask questions like that?
—A little.
—Why?
—'Cause I just do.

For the innumerable many who have not traveled with a juiced-up recorder on hand, other solutions must be considered and assessed. It's helpful to keep in mind that memoir is, first and foremost, a meditation and a quest. Conversational hints go a long way. So do suggestions. Readers don't want to plow through all those *ums* and all those pauses and all those repetitions in the service of "real life."

Nor do (most) readers want to be asked to believe that all those bons mots from childhood have been sitting somewhere, all these years, just waiting to be summoned and set down. It's disconcerting to read page upon page of conversation between a former third grader and her mother. *Really?* we readers say. *We're meant to believe this?* It's part of what gives memoir a bad rap. Readers want, at the very least, *proximity* to truth. They're expecting the acknowledgment, often implicit, that memories about conversations are the least reliable memories around. Discretion in dialogue doesn't just make for more honest memoirs. It makes for better ones.

In *No Heroes*, Chris Offutt showcases the persuasion of the short and the finely snapped. The excerpt below echoes much of the book's frank Kentucky talk. There are no breathless diatribes or monologues. Just the back-and-forth patter of regular folk:

"How's your mom and dad?" he said.
"They're all right. And yours?"

"Same. I see your mom in town, but your daddy don't hardly leave the house, does he."

"Not much," I said.

"What's he do?"

"You'll have to ask him."

In *Misgivings*, C. K. Williams uses italics to evoke remembered phrases. His italics represent a pact, a peace treaty with truth. We're not meant to believe that this was all that was said or even, perhaps, precisely what was said. Conversation is being hinted at, as is something essential and true.

> My mother and I, my mother and father and I, so much complexity, so much of what had been happiness become anguish, before it could become something else. Once, my father said to me, quietly, not unpleasantly, quite cordially in fact, coolly, in a tone as though he were complimenting me, *You're a bastard, just like your mother.*

In writing her book *Are You Somebody?: The Accidental Memoir of a Dublin Woman*, Nuala O'Faolain draws upon letters to discover who she was and how she (and a few others) phrased their thoughts in days gone past. Letters, like diary entries, operate as another kind of transcript—another variety of proof of an authentic, talking self—and when used selectively, appropriately, they enlarge a memoir's scope.

Punctuation marks signal something of the author's intent as well. Drop the quotation marks altogether and you are making less of a claim. Deploy nontraditional quotation marks and you turn the reader's gaze toward all that happens on either side of the spoken word.

There are other ways to be nontraditional, and therefore more truthful. In *Girl, Interrupted*, Susanna Kaysen strategically deploys what she comes to call "representative" conversations to depict the nature of the dialogue with the medical staff of McLean Hospital, where the author spent nearly two years in a ward for teenage girls. Kaysen's book is fast-moving, clipped. Scenes are illustrative. Exchanges are emblematic. Time is not counted; seasons are rarely named. This is what it *felt* like to be institutionalized, nearly unwittingly, at eighteen. This is how things generally sounded. Kaysen's "representative" conversations embody more truth than artificially reconstructed talk ever could.

For my own books, I have adopted the strategy best suited to the time period and topic about which I find myself writing. I don't tend to re-create childhood talk; I can't honestly say that I remember. At the same time, I don't live for insta-epiphanies—don't actively go out hunting for the topic of a next book or for memoir-worthy scenes. I don't believe that can be effectively done. But I do live paying close attention to my life, which for me entails recording my life—not just with that camera but also with diary entries and essays, with long and short blog posts, with words scribbled down on the back of a course curriculum or in the margins of a theater program. Before I ever sit down to write a book, therefore, I have within reach an accretion of both general observations and dialogue clips. I don't know why it's there, most of the time. I don't use most of it. But it exists, and I will use it if I find myself in need.

Have I always been well served by my pile of things? I am sorry to report that I have not. Have I sometimes needed conversation for a critical passage and found myself empty-handed, no recorded history in the house? Yes, of course I have. Three things have helped when such a quandary struck: the attention I pay to how people talk in general (Would she use that word? Does he talk in spurts or fluently? What does she rely on her hands to do when words fail her? Do I need to insert an *um*?), a preference for keeping most dialogue exchanges tight, and a commitment to asking those whom I am quoting to read the passages in my drafts so that they might tell me if my memory parallels theirs.

Does this produce absolute perfection? I won't claim that it does. But I do believe that if our intention is to be true, if we do all that we can to approximate the truth, if we use dialogue only when it will have the greatest impact, if we signal our relationship to dialogue (our faith in our own rendering) by the punctuation that we choose, then we are, with dialogue, doing the best that we can. And yes, at times, we memoirists are ridiculed for doing "the best that we can." Cue me in when you find a better alternative.

So we'll do the best we can. We'll practice listening. We'll practice putting talk down. Find someone to interview—your husband, your child, your neighbor, a friend—and then write a passage based on the words you wrote down. Ask them if you got it right—if you heard not just what they said but also the *way* they said it. Listen, when you're alone, to the talk of strangers. Listen to kids in the schoolyard. Listen to one end of a cell phone call. Listen to your father tell that story again. Train your ear toward the patterns of speech. You'll be glad that you did when you sit down to write memoir.

TASTES LIKE

MY mother cooked like no one else. It seemed easy for her—too easy. Her own mother had, the stories went, pitched her pies against the skinny kitchen wall on Guyer Avenue, and they had splintered spectacularly—shards, like glass. That would have never happened to my mother. Her cinnamon apples softened; her vented steam rose; her piecrust crenellated, browned, and crisped. I stole the nubs. They went down sweet.

My mother taught herself every kitchen thing—the mastery of pots, the tricks of temperature, the hidden places where bread would rise, the liquid expertise of basting brushes. She decorated her desserts with the fabric dolls that she'd sewn the night before, and if you were her child, and even if you weren't, she'd bake you three birthday cakes each year and cure you with her soup. Cooking was what my mother did because that's what she was sure mothers did. It came naturally to her, and because it did, she never recognized the colossal quality of her talent.

My mother would go to college after she raised the three of us. She'd publish her own pieces in newspapers, write books, lecture. She'd fund young artists and read thick books and collect a cavalcade of friends. All true. But when my mother died, I didn't think of that. There was only this chant in my head:

> *I will never see her eyes again.*

> *I will never have the fun of choosing a gift for her again.*

> *I will never again sit at her table.*

A way of eating passes away with your mother. How you held the sugar on your tongue. How you stirred the crumbled cheese into the oiled broth. How you savored the sweet grit of flour in the gravy pot, and the thick pink of the beef, and the heated pear with its nutmeg top, and the brownies with the confectioner's crust. You will dig through the freezer at your father's house, mad for one last frozen roll of checkerboard cookie dough, one Tupperware of thick red sauce, one crystallized slice of eggplant parmesan. You will burn your fingers with the cold. Your mother's cooking will be gone.

Or maybe it was your father who made you cream of wheat on Sunday mornings. Or maybe your sister had a trick she did with eggs. Or maybe the old man in the first-floor apartment sent you a bowl of his famous soup. Can you write beyond the gesture? Can you yield the texture and the taste? Do you know what snapped and what smooshed, what was laden down with salt, how the custard thickened, why the tomatoes off the vine were sweetest? Maybe Italian parsley means something to you. Maybe there's a story in the tip of a jalapeño pepper. Maybe the watermelon you carved into a juicy pink pig says something about the last time you saw your uncle. Maybe your neighbor's burgers, charred to a crisp, will, when you resurrect them, finally explain the shape of your nostalgia.

We can't live without eating. We're defined (they say) by what we eat. We remember the frayed cloth, the broken bread basket, the hardened cheese, the soup-thickened casserole for the hands that offered them, the way the cake was frosted, the people who gathered, the predilections and antagonisms that formed. Taste returns us to some primal part of ourselves. It sets the bridgework, the understanding, in motion. Proust taught us that. The story is familiar. No one describes it more economically than Sven Birkerts in *The Art of Time in Memoir*:

> What happened—at least according to literary legend—was that the author, revisiting as an adult one of the sites of his childhood, stopped to take tea. When he automatically dunked the crusty little cake—that famous *petite madeleine*—into his tea, he found that his unpremeditated action released a stored association of overwhelming force. A single taste suddenly swamped him with the charged-up sensation of childhood, overpowering all factual ordering, and in the light of this visceral reaction his former approaches to his remembered experience came to seem irrelevant. The vital past, the living past, he realized, could not be systematically excavated; it lay distilled in the very details that had not been groomed into story, details that could only be fortuitously discovered. The *madeleine* experience

initiated for him a whole chain of association, and from this he achieved the eventual restoration of an entire vanished world.

Tastes are pathways, then. They lead us toward story. But a meal—or a kitchen—can do even more than that for us. Jeanette Winterson had a very difficult mother. Her childhood was steeped in deprivations, brittle cold, a nearly medieval dark. But once each year Winterson's mother yielded to a mysterious celebratory tug. In *Why Be Happy When You Could Be Normal?* this sudden near-joy is gastronomically summoned. Food—its selection, its preparation—reveals character.

> We swapped our goods for smoked eel, crunchy like grated glass, and for a pudding made in cloth—a pudding made the proper way, and hard like a cannonball and speckled with fruit like a giant bird's egg. It stayed in slices when you cut it, and we poured the cherry brandy over the top and set it on fire, my dad turning the light out while my mother carried it into the parlour.

In *House of Stone*, Anthony Shadid sets a conversation about the Lebanese war against the making of a meal—*awarma*—in the kitchen of a man named Dr. Khairalla. We read of "three kilograms of meat, a glistening red," which "were the shade of cooked beets." We read that the smell of the liquefied fat was "pungent, meaty, but staler, a bit distasteful." It's death that is being discussed in the good doctor's kitchen. Massacres. The bloody meat and the pungent smell are signifiers—base, elemental—of the intimate nature of war.

We eat, and we recall our past. We cook with others, and other stories percolate between the chopping and the stirring. We watch someone we love making a meal we hope we won't forget, and something happens to us, connections are made.

In his essay "Coming Home Again," Chang-rae Lee does one of the best jobs I've ever seen of recording his mother's gestures in the kitchen—and their effect on him. It's a scene worth quoting at length, writing that I study for its specificity and tenderness. I pay special attention to Lee's verbs. I catalog all the ways he elevates this scene beyond ingredients and instructions. I take note of the single line of dialogue, and how it matters.

> I would enter the kitchen quietly and stand beside her, my chin lodging upon the point of her hip. Peering through the crook of her arm, I beheld the movements of her hands. For *kalbi*, she would take up a butchered short rib in her narrow hand, the flinty bone shaped like a section of an airplane wing and deeply embedded in gristle and flesh, and with the point of her knife cut so that the bone fell away, though not completely, leaving it connected to the meat by the barest opaque layer of tendon. Then she methodically butterflied the flesh, cutting and unfolding, repeating the action until the meat lay out on her board, glistening and ready for seasoning. She scored it diagonally, then sifted sugar into the crevices with her pinched fingers,

gently rubbing in the crystals. The sugar would tenderize as well as sweeten the meat. She did this with each rib, and then set them all aside in a large shallow bowl. She minced a half-dozen cloves of garlic, a stub of gingerroot, sliced up a few scallions, and spread it all over the meat. She wiped her hands and took out a bottle of sesame oil, and, after pausing for a moment, streamed the dark oil in two swift circles around the bowl. After adding a few splashes of soy sauce, she thrust her hands in and kneaded the flesh, careful not to dislodge the bones. I asked her why it mattered that they remain connected. "The meat needs the bone nearby," she said, "to borrow its richness." She wiped her hands clean of the marinade, except for her little finger, which she would flick with her tongue from time to time, because she knew that the flavor of a good dish developed not at once but in stages.

Virginia Woolf once wrote, in *A Room of One's Own*, that novelists "have a way of making us believe that luncheon parties are invariably memorable for something very witty that was said, or for something very wise that was done. But they seldom spare a word for what was eaten." I feel the same way about memoirs. Not those memoirs written specifically about kitchens or about food, or amplified by recipes. Not, in other words, M. F. K. Fisher, Anthony Bourdain, Ruth Reichl, Gabrielle Hamilton, and all the others. I'm talking everything else—the memoirs about childhood, love, or grief; the memoirs about going away and coming back; the memoirs about loss or illness. Where are the kitchen smells and treats? Where is the oven's simmering heat, or the trail of excess flour, or the permanent char on the lip of the pan, or the basil snipped from the pot on the sill?

We have to slow down to remember those details. We have to trust that writing ourselves back to the dining room at midnight or the campfire at dusk or the charcoal grill across the fence is going to take us somewhere new, forge a bright and unexpected connection, be finally integral to the greater pattern that we are tracing.

When my mother passed away, my father bestowed two gifts: the photo album that she had given to him as an early Christmas present (the cover is wood, the pages are black, the black-and-white square photographs are captioned with white pencil) and her original recipe book. I treasure both things more than any other possible maternal thing. They are what I didn't lose when I lost her.

As I write this chapter, my mother's recipe book spills across my smudged glass desk—the jaws of its three-ring permanently agape, the punched holes of the notebook paper torn through, the brightly named divider pages—Preserving, Salads, Fruits, Meats, Vegetables—delivering nothing of the sort. There's no order here, and I suspect there never was. There is, instead, a profusion of cellophaned newspaper recipes, magazine clippings, coupons, grocery store recipe cards, handwritten notes (the ink now more gray than blue, most of it splattered and diffused), one invitation to a Sloan School Bon Voyage Brunch, and a single sheet of arithmetic problems she must have written out for me so that she could frost a cake or tenderize a sirloin. My math that day got done on a Sun Oil Company calculation sheet. Above the problems, she'd made this note: *Beth. 5 years old.*

Pancake Crisps. Feathery Fudge Cake. Fresh-as-a-Daisy
Cake. Date-Nut Coffee Cake. Cheese-Olive Rings. Old-
Fashioned Spicy Oat Cake. Heavenly Pumpkin Pie. Saucy
Cupcakes. Lovelight Teacakes. Orange Chiffon Pie. Picnic
Spice Cake. Good Traveler Birthday Cake. Savory Broiled
Flank Steak. Carnation Burgers-on-a-Stick. Rodeo Rings.
Rolled Chicken Washington. Salmon Patties. Tiny Stuffed
Tomatoes. Foil-Blanketed Franks. Sausage Ring with
Scrambled Eggs. Snowflake Cake: Good/Moist. Careful not
to crack the hardened tape or bruise the yellowed pages, I
move through my mother's recipes like an archaeologist—
trying to imagine but incapable of fully imagining all the
hours she must have sat on her kitchen stool searching for
clues to our next meal, our coming birthday extravaganza.
My mother wanted to read. She wanted to write. But this,
mostly, is what she did, what she felt herself responsible for.
I suspect we didn't thank her nearly enough. I don't have a
chance to thank her now.

Brownies. The page is handwritten. The page is tarnished.

1 c. sugar
3 tspns. cocoa
2 eggs, slightly building
1 tspn van
¾ c flour
6 ttspns butter, melted

Mix sugar cocoa. Add eggs and vanilla, beat until
smooth, stir in flour, add butter and mix well. Bake
in 8 x 8". About 30 minutes.

There's no more than this—no hints about temperature,
no indication as to whether that double *t* in front of the

butter is an in-haste error or a secret sign. Still, when my father comes to dinner, or when Thanksgiving hurries close, or if I'm missing my mother, I will take out this page and make these brownies, experimenting each time, just a little. My brownies never come out like her brownies came out. They are never as luscious or moist. The thin ceiling of chocolate cracks beneath the weight of white sugar. The edges stick to the pan. I sit down wanting to find, somehow, my mother, but I find only me looking for her.

I cannot make my mother's brownies like my mother made her brownies, but I can try. I cannot materially re-create a meal with words, but in sinking in with the attempt, in trying to locate the snatch of my childhood, I am shortening the distance between now and so many thens. I am rousing memory; I am working toward meaning. If we stand in the kitchen long enough, if we pursue the sugar trail of our early years, if we stop and notice now how the chocolate curls and the carrots whimper and the hand stirs and beats and frosts, we will have given ourselves the gift of greater content and deeper knowing. We will be made closer to whole, and closer to whole is nudging closer to having something true to say.

SOMETHING SMELLS . . . FISHY?

NOT long ago, my father decided to take me back home, to the first house he'd ever owned. He'd bought the corner-lot split-level in 1957 for $14,000 with help from the GI Bill. He'd worked just a few miles away at an oil refinery where, as a chemical engineer, he helped thwart fires, build a catalytic converter, and manage sudden flares. There was no phone in that house; my mother walked miles to call her mother. There was a backyard sandbox; a neighbor whose house I remember for a single detail, blue; and a sidewalk that seemed to magnetize ants, especially when I sat upon it, chalking.

My father, my husband, and I set out on our adventure relying on my father's GPS, which never quite manages (in my father's car) to deliver the promised pronto magic. We went on and off the wrong highways until we got to the right one and turned into Ashbourne Hills, a neighborhood that, from above, might look like a child's Spirograph construction—bulbously looped with returns, all the houses the same except in the small ways that they are different.

This is the one, my father finally announced, pulling up to a corner house and parking the car. I hadn't been to

Ashbourne Hills since I'd left as a child of three, but it didn't feel right. I snapped a photograph, nevertheless, suspicious. Something about the angle seemed off. Something about the sun and the size of the front-yard tree. And something—how can I explain this?—about the way the old place *smelled*.

Dad, I finally said. *This isn't home.*

And it wasn't, as it turned out. Home was two blocks north, a similarly styled corner, an equidistant setback, a modest simulacrum of the other brick-based split-level. Home was (sure, I'm animal-crazy) a different smell. Something about the trees, perhaps, in the neighbor's yard. Some hint of honeysuckle coming.

They call it olfaction. They talk about sensory nerves, cilia, basal cells, odor receptors, and odorant molecules, but we know better. We know that it's the brackish marsh grass at the edge of the dune that levers us toward our memories of Stone Harbor. We know it's the slightly woodsy smell of the nut beads we find in a child's macramé bracelet that returns us to Sun Oil Day Camp the year our arm was in a cast. We know the smell of plaster takes us back to that full-arm, itchy-as-all-hell cast, and we know that it's the smell of bleach in a mop bucket that returns us to the hospital where we lay with our smashed arm, waiting for the surgeon to arrive. *What is that smell?* we'll wonder, and somewhere deep within our dendrite morphology the lights go on, the electricity sparks, the chemistry goes zinging. Baby powder. Wet sticks. Car exhaust. Burned rubber. Gym mats. Locker rooms. An old wool hat. The asbestos lining in an attic. Pine needles. Lavender. Spray paint. The metallic charge between a hammer and a nail. Smell, like a lasso, takes hold. Sit with it awhile, and you'll know.

What can you smell? What smells transport you? What smells do you associate with childhood, and why, and how has time interceded, and how, in some mysterious way, has time not passed at all? Here are Dorothy Allison, Marie Arana, Eudora Welty, and Vladimir Nabokov on the trail of odorants. Think, as you read, about your own ol' factory.

Where I was born—Greenville, South Carolina— smelled like nowhere else I've ever been. Cut wet grass, split green apples, baby shit and beer bottles, cheap makeup and motor oil. Everything was ripe, everything was rotting. —Dorothy Allison, *Two or Three Things I Know for Sure*

The corridors of my skull are haunted. I carry the smell of sugar there. The odors of a factory—wet cane, dripping iron, molasses pits—are up behind my forehead, deep inside my throat. I'm reminded of those scents when children offer me candy from a damp palm, when the man I love sighs with wine upon his tongue, when I inhale the heartbreaking sweetness of rotting fruit and human waste that rises from garbage dwellers' camps along the road to Lima. —Marie Arana, *American Chica*

In a children's art class, we sat in a ring on kinder-garten chairs and drew three daffodils that had just been picked out of the yard; and while I was draw-ing, my sharpened yellow pencil and the cup of the yellow daffodil gave off whiffs just alike. That the pencil doing the drawing should give off the same smell as the flower it drew seemed part of the art lesson—as shouldn't it be? —Eudora Welty, *One Writer's Beginnings*

Mademoiselle's room, both in the country and in town, was a weird place to me—a kind of hothouse sheltering a thick-leaved plant imbued with a heavy, enuretic odor. Although next to ours, when we were small, it did not seem to belong to our pleasant, well-aired home. In that sickening mist, reeking, among other woolier effluvia, of the brown smell of oxidized apple peel, the lamp burned low, and strange objects glimmered upon the writing desk: a lacquered box with licorice sticks, black segments of which she would hack off with her penknife and put to melt under her tongue; a picture postcard of a lake . . . —Vladimir Nabokov, *Speak, Memory*

Easy prompt for a stuck writing day: Choose a smell, and write into it your story. It's the cracked pepper on the fried egg. It's the smell of fresh tar on a driveway. It's the strawberry pendant above the fresh-shredded mulch. It's the rot of an orange in a bowl. It's cat pee on a rug. It's the smell inside your oldest book. It's the basement smell after rain. It's Crest toothpaste, lemon Lysol, Ivory soap, melting wax, your mother's perfume, the bottom of your knapsack, nail polish, sawdust, fly strips, coin collections, the cardboard molt of an actual old-time record, the carcass in the spiderweb. One of them is yours, or something else is.

There are smells out there that explain you. There are smells that take you home.

EMPTY YOUR POCKETS

SOMETIMES I ask my students to empty their pockets and to put everything right out there, on the table. No pockets? They dig into their backpacks or purses. And if somehow (too strangely, not rightly) all they have in their possession are their laptops, I ask them to close their eyes and think for a moment about the things they left back in their rooms, stuffed in a desk drawer or perched on a windowsill.

What are you carrying forward? I ask them. What are you keeping close?

Here are but a few things that have been placed upon our altar:

- keys (of course)

- the essential modern-day paper and plastic (license, work ID, health insurance cards, library cards, the yogurt-shop card with the eight punch holes)

- every conceivable brand of smartphone

- bills and coins

- parking tickets

- a chipped seashell

- a pocket-crushed feather

- a fake pack of gum (don't ask me; it was there)

- a toothbrush (owner of which had a killer smile)

- a hairbrush (apparently unused)

- a nail file (needing replacement)

- a pale pink comb

- recipe cards

- photographs

- a pack of raisins

- books (dog-eared, even)

- sparkly glitter pens

- rub-on tattoos

I could go on. I won't. The point is what happens next. Choose the thing that matters most, I say. Choose the thing that is so much more than the sum of its parts, so much more than its self-apparent, pragmatic function; choose the thing freighted with meaning. Which one do you keep close *just because*? Which one, when push comes to shove, is *irreplaceable*? I wait. Deciding can take awhile. But when it's clear that choices have been made, I get the students writing. Define *irreplaceable*, I say. Then tell me about irreplaceable by writing your chosen object's story.

The answers are moving, surprising, often funny. They tell me (they tell others) so much about the person sitting there, what he values and how he sees, how he measures things, one against the other. This is irreplaceable because my mother gave it to me. This is irreplaceable because no other comb that I've ever found has such soft, even subtle teeth. This is irreplaceable because it took me three years and six holidays' worth of trying to get my grandmother to reveal her tomato sauce secret, and if I lose the card I wrote her ingredients on, she will never trust me again in the kitchen. This shell is irreplaceable because my brother found it for me in the year I could not travel to the ocean. These photographs were found in a Ziploc bag after the flood in my parents' basement.

Now, I say, write about something that *has* been lost. Something you didn't think you could live without. Write about absence. Write about search. Write about reconciling yourself to the idea of something eternally missing. What is the language of loss? How does one resurrect the thing that can no longer be held, touched, seen, corresponded with? Are words replacements? Can they be made to be? How is the approximating work of a writer deeply frustrating and deeply satisfying? Why does writing always feel like almost or nearly, and why do we keep trying anyway? What impels us?

What impels you?

Diversion by way of example: We moved to the house where I now live close to twenty years ago. In the course of planning the move, I set every material thing that actually mattered to me into two cardboard boxes. The dolls my father would bring home to me following his travels abroad. The collection of Hummel figurines I had acquired as a child, one by one, as I, too, began to see the world. The Venetian masks, leather wrought, that my husband and I had discovered in a corner store in a day of thick fog on a street we were never, in subsequent travels, in miles of walking, able to find again. My porcelain dogs, an inch high at most—substitutes for the real puppy I'd always wanted. A few long-maned china horses.

These were talismans; these were evidence. These were proof of being loved and having loved. I treasured these things deeply. Entombed them with newspaper and padding. Put them inside the sturdiest boxes. Asked the moving men to carry them forward in a special part of the truck. Waited, anxious, to see them again. I never saw them again. Somehow these things had gone missing.

It's been twenty years, as I have said, and I'm still not used to the idea of so much missing. I still find myself on my knees in the attic dust, digging through piles and papers and crates—as if looking hard enough will solve this crime of absence. It doesn't. My masks are still gone, and my puppies, the little Hummel girl with the frozen, windswept hair that I bought with all the money I had as a nine-year-old in a German shop. My special treasures never made it to the home where I live now. The home feels partial, less than.

I don't have the things, but I write toward them.

Just as I write toward the grandmother I lost, the uncle I lost, my mother. Just as I write toward—we all write toward—childhood. Just as, in my Salvador memoir, I wrote toward a place called Santa Tecla, my husband's home, which was dusted down to nothing by a seismic earthquake just as

I was finishing the book. "Words are the weights that hold our histories in place," I wrote then and I believe ever more firmly now, and as memoirists our job is to understand not just what we are holding in place but also why. Why does it matter so much that we try? Will we be able to live with the foreordained imperfections? Can our quest to keep what cannot be kept signify for another?

Empty your pockets. Know what you value. Write it down so that I can see it, want it, nearly touch it, too. So that I will yearn with you, or so that I can mourn with you, because loss is now, or loss is coming, and loss is our shared human condition. You have never seen my Venetian masks, and I have never cooked your grandmother's red sauce. But if we both write most truly, we will enable each other's compassion.

Memoir commands us to engender compassion.

TELLING DETAIL

I most likely would not have fallen so hard for memoir—
or had the guts to try to write it—had I not happened upon
Natalie Kusz's miraculous *Road Song* in a Princeton, New
Jersey, bookstore in 1990. The story of the author's long
recovery from the ferocious attack of a pack of Alaskan
dogs, *Road Song* was, for me, the revelation of a form. Here
was the past delivered with equanimity and respect. Here
was a terrible tragedy gentled by words, a book in which
the good is ever equal to the bad. Kusz wrote to comprehend, and not to condemn. She wrote her way back to
herself, and as she did, she broadened the reader's perspective, disassembled bitterness, healed. *Road Song* begins in
the spirit of adventure, not with despair. It begins with an
our and not an *I* and reverberates out, like a hymn. There is
no selling out here. Just a hand reaching out across the
page.

I blame Natalie Kusz.

Not yet published, entirely unschooled as a writer (so
unschooled that I had yet to meet a *real* writer, let alone
converse with one), I wrote to Kusz at her publisher's address. This was during that great, unrivaled epoch of

letters, stamps, blue-ink signatures. This was that time when hovering by my mailbox required going outside, into the weather, getting hot or getting wet. It was early December when Kusz's letter arrived. I have it right here in a frame. It reads, in part:

> As I am sure you know . . . writers are in the business of attempting to expose the human condition in such a way that our description resonates in the souls of other humans, and it is extremely gratifying to hear about the one or two times when something we publish succeeds in this endeavor.

I have carried this letter everywhere. I have returned to it time and again. I hadn't read memoir, hadn't written it, and then there was Kusz unveiling its mystery for me, explaining, by way of a thank-you, what a book like hers was designed to do. *Writers are in the business of attempting to expose the human condition in such a way that our description resonates in the souls of other humans. . . .* Yes, I thought. I want to be in that business.

Road Song was my first instruction. It is a book I hold incalculably dear. And it is a book that I sometimes read out loud to the students who come to that Victorian manse and sit around the thick, old, patient table. I read from the harrowing early pages, when Kusz, then a little girl, is walking home from school with her dog, Hobo. Her mother is not home, and so Kusz carries on, toward a neighbor. Dogs pace and growl between where she is and where she wants to be—huskies tethered to their chains. They're agitated, restless. The snow, in places, is taller than the girl herself. It is Alaska cold. Kusz calls out to quiet the dogs, calls out to find courage herself, and when the boy she is looking for also isn't home, when she turns and walks the slender spit of ground between the doghouses and the howling dogs, when she finally makes her way to the end of that dog madness and allows herself to feel grateful for her own courage, she, well, here—let Kusz tell you for herself:

I was walking past the last dog and I felt brave, and I forgave him and bent to lay my mitten on his head. He surged forward on a chain much longer than I thought, leaping at my face, catching my hair in his mouth, shaking it in his teeth until the skin gave way with a jagged sound. My feet were too slow in my boots, and as I blundered backward they tangled in the chain, burning my legs on metal. I called out at Paul's window, expecting rescue, angry that it did not come, and I beat my arms in front of me, and the dog was back again, pulling me down.

A hole was worn into the snow, and I fit into it, arms and legs drawn up in front of me. The dog snatched and pulled at my mouth, eyes, hair; his breath clouded the air around us, but I did not feel its heat, or smell the blood sinking down between hairs of his muzzle. I watched my mitten come off in his teeth and sail upward, and it seemed unfair then and very sad that one hand should freeze all alone; I lifted the second mitten off and threw it away, then turned my face back again, overtaken suddenly by loneliness. A loud river ran in my ears, dragging me under.

This passage remains for me one of the most devastating scenes in all of memoir. I can never read it aloud without pausing to catch my breath, to wipe away a tear. What happened to Natalie Kusz is, of course, a tragedy. With simple language, with supreme clarity, without self-pity, Kusz enables us to see and to feel the puncture of untamed teeth, the lonely assault.

But when I ask my students what makes this passage so searing, so perfect and perfectly terrifying, it is, of course, that mitten, tossed: ". . . it seemed unfair then and very sad that one hand should freeze all alone; I lifted the second mitten off and threw it away . . ." The mitten tells us everything. The mitten—which is not blood, which is not teeth, which is not pain, which is not, then, *overt*—is the trembling heart of this devastating story. It is why we ultimately feel Kusz's pain as profoundly as we do.

The telling detail. We know one when we see one. We recognize the pattern. Foreground/background. Here it is, again. The main action of this story is howling dogs and a lonesome walk by a little girl. The signifier—the flag, the surrender—is the mitten.

"When you write, you lay out a line of words," Annie Dillard has written. "The line of words is a miner's pick, a woodcarver's gouge, a surgeon's probe. You wield it, and it digs a path you follow. Soon you find yourself deep in new territory. Is it a dead end, or have you located the real subject? You will know tomorrow, or this time next year."

Follow the line of your own words. Follow the lines set

down by others. Hunt down the telling detail. Here is a passage from the not-quite-a-memoir known as *Say Her Name*, by Francisco Goldman. You don't need to know anything more about it, just now, except that it reads like this:

> I had a friend, Saqui, who'd covered more war than anyone my age I knew: Afghanistan, Africa, and the Middle East, as well as Central America. Saqui told me about walking out of his hotel on Avenida Reforma the night he got to Mexico City, two nights after the quake, the air thick with smog, pulverized cement, and acrid smoke, and how, when he was crossing the avenue, he saw, in one of the lanes closed off to traffic, a dead child laid out on the pavement, a little girl in sweatshirt, jeans, and sneakers, who looked like she'd been rolled in flour. There were two Mexican men standing over her, and my friend told me that they looked at him in a way that so sorrowfully but menacingly warned him not to come any closer that he swerved away as if they were pointing guns, not daring even to glance back until he'd crossed onto the opposite sidewalk, where he turned and saw the two men still standing over the little corpse as if they were waiting for a bus, and he thought it was the saddest, most terrible thing he'd ever seen.

Read it through again. Mark out those details that make this passage vivid, memorable. I'll wager that the reference to flour—so simple, so primal, so right—has been noted. I'll imagine that the way the two men stood by the girl, the way they looked "as if they were pointing guns" stopped you, too—made you more capable of imagining the scene. Imagination and empathy are near cousins. Writers who help us see clearly, who make room for us beside them, will likely earn our compassion, and our time. Neither Kusz nor Goldman relies on ornate gestures or complicated schemas. Their images are organic, grasped in an instant. Mitten as surrender. A child rolled in flour.

So close your eyes now, and lean back. Direct your thoughts toward the first childhood room that you can remember. Take stock. Where is the light coming from? What is in that toy box on the floor? Why are the picture books double-stacked, and what happened to the stuffed clown's nose, and why is there a half-dollar coin stuck in the piggy bank slot? Did you choose the white dresser for yourself, or was it borrowed? Did you write your own name on the wall? Did your brother break the wooden horse? Did your mother rock in that chair?

Take your time; nobody's rushing you. Let it all come back, as memories do. Faulty, surely. An estimate, of course. Still, and nonetheless, do what you can.

Then find a pencil.

Then find a page.

(Please walk away from the computer. Please?)

And write.

Write what you remember, what you feel as you remember, what you wish that you could see but can't. Then look at the words that you have laid down, in those first lines—the pick, the gouge, the probe—and isolate your most telling, most signifying, and therefore most complete detail. On a new page, with a sharpened pencil, write the detail better. Look for wasteland stretches that might be eradicated, flat horizons in need of sky, opportunities to turn complication into complexity. Ask yourself, *Is this the best that I can do?* Do nothing less when writing memoir.

LET ME CHECK ON THAT

RESEARCH is subterranean; it's submersion. It dirties you up, challenges your presumptions, broadens your spectrum. It offers a defense against the faultiness of memory and against critics such as Ben Yagoda, who in *Memoir* delights in reminding the rememberers that their pastime is practically feckless: "Among the most lasting of Freud's many revolutionary insights concerned the capriciousness of memory. . . . In experiment after experiment, study after study, subsequent psychologists have gone a good deal farther, establishing that memory is by nature untrustworthy: contaminated not merely by gaps, but by distortions and fabrications that inevitably and blamelessly creep into it."

Our memories will fail us; there's no pretending they won't. We'll get things wrong, and not just the talk. We'll be contradicted, doubted, pilloried maybe. Research helps—not just in after-the-fact self-defense but also in the original priming of the story. Absent the stark scribble of case file documents, how could Susanna Kaysen have so effectively pieced together the life she'd lived in that mental institution? How could she, in *Girl, Interrupted*, have convinced herself (first) and her readers (second) just what happened on the morning that the physician committed her to an inmate life in an asylum? We need to know who to believe—the doctor or Kaysen. By digging out the admission note of April 27, 1967, by reproducing it in the pages of her book, Kaysen finds her way to the most accurate possible rendering of that harrowing moment. She puts us on her side.

Where would Mary Karr have been without her sister's corrective memory (or the threat of it) as she set out to write *The Liars' Club*? What would we think (or care to believe) had Anthony Shadid, an acclaimed journalist, not paid such close attention to the researchable facts—about the war in and against the Middle East, about his Lebanese ancestors—even as he wrote his very personal story, *House of Stone*? Sometimes research *is* the story, as memoir becomes the *investigation* of one's life. Such was the case for Ned Zeman, the *Vanity Fair* reporter who, following a succession of increasingly violent treatments for violent depression, finds himself an amnesiac fitting together the puzzle of his life, one frayed cardboard piece after another. His *Rules of the Tunnel*, like *House of Prayer No. 2*, is a "you" story. It is also proof of the power of the undercover-cop memoir. What happened to me? How did it happen?

From the prologue of *The Rules of the Tunnel*:

The void stretched back for months, maybe a year, save for random bits (JetBlue potato chips) and pieces (tiny pink shoes) signifying nothing. The rest of the story would have to come by way of shoe leather and notepads. Which made you, in addition to the world's first amnesiac reporter, appreciative of why monkeys don't become airline pilots. You were the worst subject you'd ever interviewed (and the feeling was mutual). You felt deceived, stonewalled; you felt ambushed, persecuted. You wanted to sue yourself for libel.

Like Zeman, *New York Times* columnist David Carr and *New York Post* reporter Susannah Cahalan had to hunt for the small and large details of their own lives to concretize the facts. Carr was, by his own admission, a thug, an addict, and an abuser before he sobered up, plucked his children free of welfare, and became the *Times* fixture he now is. Cahalan was living her life—a good job, a bright boyfriend—when an undiagnosed autoimmune disease radically redefined her health and put her future at risk. Neither Carr nor Cahalan could, independently, remember much of what happened. Reportage was their out. Their respective memoirs—*The Night of the Gun* and *Brain on Fire*—are unearthed memoirs. Research *is* the story.

Of course, the scenario needn't be so extreme for research to elevate memoir. When I wrote memoir, I was, of course, writing my life. But I was also following the always persistent, hardly consistent, rarely well-tiled path of my insatiable curiosity. If I was writing about friendships—my own—I was also writing about, or at least wondering about, the history of friendship, the word as defined by Cicero and Montaigne and Francine du Plessix Gray, the rareness of the relationship, the conclusions other writers have drawn—in memoirs, in novels, in psychological research. I was writing about what I remembered and what I came to know. I was reaching for the greater world even as I told my personal story.

Say, for example, that I was writing about my marriage to a Salvadoran man, that I was pursuing the question *How well do we ever really know the people we've come to love?* I had, in my head, the SparkNotes version of my one and only marriage romance, which is to say the mess and wild tussle of what it feels like to fall in love, be in love, fight to stay in love. I could—without ever leaving my chair, without tapping a single keyboard key, without picking up a book, without interviewing another person—give you the love goods. But if I had written a book like that, I'd have been a capital-M *Me* speaking without the graces of enriched perspective. I'd have been, in other words, a narcissistic bore.

I wanted to write a story that mattered. I wanted, besides, to learn about my husband's country, El Salvador. The land itself, the coffee farms, the grandfather my husband loved, the guerrilla warfare that fractured his world, the divisions of earth and politics. There would be, I trusted, wisdom in all of that. Life lessons. Metaphors. I would grow not just as a writer but also as a person and as a wife. I would dig until I finally commanded some part of that Salvadoran family and world as my own. Until I, in some small ways, fit in. Until I lost my outsider status. I would come to think harder about bridges, cleaving, foreignness. I would find room for myself, and room for my readers, in a story about marriage, strangeness, and war. I would establish myself within the tangled life web and make some relatable sense of it all.

But it would take time. The old family photographs

had to be found. The antique pamphlets on coffee farming.
The textbooks on plate tectonics. The wildlife guides. The
history of the Brazilian who brought coffee to El Salvador
in the first place. The stained and crumbling newspaper
stories. The political interviews. The Carolyn Forché poems. The photographs I took when hiking the jungle hills
alone, or when walking lost near dusk along an estuary, or
when escaping the bombs that I'd just been told would
soon explode in the capital city. Even if I didn't know my
husband's primary language, Spanish, I listened for all that
lay within its rhythms and oscillating volume. I sought out
the aunt who would speak English with me. I asked questions of the brothers. I matched the stories they told against
the faded news journals that I read, and I built, small bit by
small bit, the story.

What do your hard facts imply? What do they teach
you about the story? What do they offer in terms of analogy
and depth? I had to write the land of El Salvador—and the
way the land itself was made—before I could truly come to
understand all that separated my husband from me, all that
makes him so exotically different, so artistically foreign, so
finally lovely.

In the hooting, crawling, philandering shade of an
overgrown jungle, high, near the sky, it is possible
to imagine that the world is as the world always
was. This is illusion, the chicanery of nature. For
when it comes to Central America, to El Salvador,
to St. Anthony's Farm, there was indeed a time, as
the Maya say, when the sky seemed crashed against
the earth, when there was darkness only, nothing

at all. The land that forms Central America is erupted earth, the aftereffect of spectacular geological discontent, a land bridge suffering the wind and weather of two barely separated seas. Sixty million years ago, there was only ocean where the land bridge lies today. Eleven million years ago, there was but a single archipelago. Having risen from the volcanic sea in fits of calm and violence, that archipelago would be joined, over the course of many more millions of years, by additional by-products of glaciation and geological turbulence until the isthmian sill grew deeper and more and more land poked its nose up to the sky. The islands wouldn't connect, the pocked, swamped, peaking, dipping hissing isthmian barrier wouldn't be complete, until three million years ago. But the cross-pollination of North and South American life was already in the works, so Central America was from the first an incubator of the exotic and inexplicable. —*Still Love in Strange Places*

Research is alivedness. It is the rush of something new and unexpected. It keeps you engaged, in suspense, full of the unprotected *what if*s. Research requires us to shed our comfortable conceits, to break the formulae, to scramble the math. You didn't see that metaphor coming? Fantastic news. You were brazenly sure that the front door on the old house on Guyer Avenue was red until somebody showed you the photographs? Good. What else don't you know, and why don't you know it, and is uncertainty part of your story? The big pile of papers that someone just sent you has messed with your sanguinity and self-assurance, your confidence, your frame? All right, then. You're getting close. That interview you just completed—the one that contradicts the interview you conducted last week, the one you thought for sure was the Final Word? Perfect. Yes. You see it now. This memoir business is messier than you thought. Messier and far more interesting.

Research will never, however, be fully compensatory. Research isn't, in the end, plenary. You could research for years, exhaust all the documents, relentlessly interview the myriad eyewitnesses, undergird your memoir with film reels and photographs, and you would still be confuted and resisted; you would be refuted; you would question yourself. I spent those fifteen years writing about marriage and El Salvador. I bought every book I thought there was. I talked to every family member who would speak to me. I picked coffee beneath jungle shade, watched the *campesinos* sort red beans from green, asked my husband, again and again, to tell me that story one more time. I called my brother-in-law, the one then living in Dallas. I called the one who had made his family home in Spain. I asked my son, after we had traveled to El Salvador and back again, *Did you see what I saw?*

And as true as I believed my memoir to be—as true as I have been told, by all those family members, that it is—I not too long ago sat with my husband and his family while they searched through the old photo albums again. They brought the long gone back again, close. They told their stories as if for the first time. I sat chin to my knees across from that couch and listened as they hovered and exclaimed. It was the nuances that changed—the gift that had been brought to the party, perhaps, or the hour in the day. There were debates about who had seen what first, or who had hidden a secret for a day. *It wasn't like that, it was like this,* they said among themselves, and I thought of my book on the shelf, the words fixed in their place. I thought of how stories mutate with time, and with the teller, even the stories confidently set down in ink.

Research is corroborating, substantiating, authenticating; it, too, bears witness. But certain facts will remain elusive, or they will change with time. At some point, we have to trust what we have and what we can make of what we have. We can be absolutely sure of just one thing in all of this: that our hearts are true throughout the making of our story.

FIRST MEMORY

TAKE stock. You have opinions, now, about tense and form. You've sifted photographs, listened to talk, remembered kitchens, sunk into your stinky-sweet olfaction. You've emptied your pockets and written loss. You've resurrected a childhood room, a telling detail. You've come to know more about the ways you see and think, the ways you process and remember and auction off the facts, the ways you live weather, landscape, song, and hue. You've read memoir (please tell me you've read memoir) and clarified (at least a bit) what it is you expect from your memoir self. It's time for one more exercise. Relax. Nobody's looking.

I want you—you saw this coming—to write your first memory. I'm not going to lie: This won't be easy. You're going to flail. Let yourself flail. You're going to ask yourself: Is this true? Is this right? Does this matter? Go with your fears; memoir is nothing if not frightening. Turn off the phone; first memories shouldn't be interrupted. Find the old photographs, if you have them. Find that scrapbook your mother kept, or that fishing reel your father left you, or that box of toys that's still in your uncle's attic, or the ornaments from the early Christmas tree, or the book your grandmother read you. And if you don't have these things, it's all right. Exhale. You have your neurons and dendrites, your prions that some scientists believe mark out memories in the brain.

You have time. Roll through it.

Fear finds its way into my first memory. Fear and a blue-sky afternoon in that cul-de-sac of 1950s-era houses—my parents' first neighborhood, the one I only just recently (but barely) found. For the first time, I am bearing witness to a crime—an assault against the pretty plastic streamers on the handlebars of my older brother's bike. Like teeth, the streamers have been yanked out, one by one, and now nothing flies, nothing tinsels when the bike wheels go forward. Who would have done such a thing, and why? How could anybody dare hurt my brother? And where is he, and does he know yet, and can my mother fix this? I see myself—my feet planted on the snaking concrete-tile walk—incapable of moving, impossibly sad, distraught. I don't have the words for betrayal, not yet. I don't know what justice is, so how can I form thoughts of its opposite? But I am confused, and the confusion is electrifying, and so are my inchoate feelings for my brother: *This should not have happened to him.*

Elias Canetti's first memory is, as he writes in *The Tongue Set Free*, "dipped in red."

> I come out of a door on the arm of a maid, the floor in front of me is red, and to the left a staircase goes down, equally red. Across from us, at the same height, a door opens, and a smiling man steps forth, walking towards me in a friendly way. He steps right up close to me, halts, and says: "Show me

your tongue." I stick out my tongue, he reaches into his pocket, pulls out a jackknife, opens it, and brings the blade all the way to my tongue. He says: "Now we'll cut off his tongue." I don't dare pull back my tongue, he comes closer and closer, the blade will touch me any second. In the last moment, he pulls back the knife, saying: "Not today, tomorrow." He snaps the knife shut again and puts it back in his pocket.

Every morning, we step out of the door and into the red hallway, the door opens, and the smiling man appears. I know what he's going to say and I wait for the command to show my tongue. I know he's going to cut it off, and I get more and more scared each time. That's how the day starts, and it happens very often.

A first memory born of a raw, unsettling, ungraspable emotion. Another first memory born of color (and seductive terror). Here, in *Cakewalk*, is an early memory born quite specifically of sweets. Kate Moses, the memoir's author, is "not quite four" when she heads across the street to play for the first time with a neighbor girl. A cake has been set out on the new friend's kitchen counter. It beckons, and no parents are in sight. Kate encourages her playmate to take "just one taste." Soon the entire cake is gone.

What was that? I was thinking as I burst out the neighbor girl's front door and skittered across her lawn, her mother still on the phone shrieking to my mother, my sticky hair flying behind me and my stiff new dress flapping, my mother erupting out of our house across the street and running toward me, a look of abject mortification on her heart-shaped face.

I knew I had been very bad. I knew I was going to be punished, maybe even spanked. But I didn't care. Whatever it was, whatever that voluptuous thing was, it had been worth it. *What was it?* I was still wondering later, after my father had come home. That baked thing, that glazed and golden and sumptuous thing—I wanted it again. And again. And again. I lay on my bed, my bottom sore, sucking the last ambrosial flavor from my candied hair.

In *Limbo*, a book about a young pianist struck down by a mysterious muscle disorder, A. Manette Ansay suggests that her first memory "is of memory itself—and the fear of its loss, that vast outer dark."

One night, as I lay floating in the still, dark pond between wakefulness and sleep, a stray thought breached the surface like a fish. *You will forget this.* I opened my eyes. To my right, tucked under the covers beside me, was an eyeless Raggedy Ann doll. To my left, on top of the covers, was a large plastic spark plug—a display model that my father, a traveling salesman, had coaxed from some far dealership and presented to me. My father's gifts were unpredictable and strange: hotel ashtrays, pens with company slogans trailing down their sides, desiccated frogs and snakes he found along the highway, jaws

pulled back in agonized smiles. These things populated the bedroom I shared with my two-year-
old brother like the grasshoppers and pianos and
clocks in a Dali painting, startling the eye from my
mother's homemade curtains, the Infant of Prague
night-light keeping watch on the bedside table, the
child-size rocking chair. The spark plug was nearly
three feet long; if you shook it, something mysterious rattled around inside. It was tied to a wooden
spool and, during the day, I dragged it clattering
after me, the way other girls carried dolls.

You will forget this.

It was 1969. I was four years old, almost five.
The thought swam back and forth in the darkness,
gaining speed . . .

Something Wordsworthian factors into Priscilla Gilman's first memory. Thunder. A father. A conquering of
fear. She tells the story in *The Anti-Romantic Child*:

It was a summer night in Spain, I was a little over
three, and an especially dramatic thunderstorm
woke me, terrified, in the middle of the night. The
memory begins with my father's voice in my ear
and the two of us gazing out into the night. Framed
by the large window, the scene before us was like
a little theater: the familiar garden strangely unfamiliar, the sky an indigo blue lit periodically by silvery flashes. Narrating the scene, my father sounded
like a madcap sportscaster. "There's a big lightning!
There's a little one . . . oh a big one again!" he ex

claimed as he held me firmly with one hand and gesticulated skyward with the other. I remember something disorienting becoming something glorious. I remember feeling so safe not because he protected me from fear but because he helped me to confront it.

In *All the Strange Hours*, Loren Eiseley recalls a conversation with W. H. Auden, in which the poet asked Eiseley what public event he remembered first from childhood. It's not the sinking of the *Titanic*, which Auden reveals to be his own spark point. It is, Eiseley reveals, a story that involves "a warden, a prison, and a blizzard." Time and again (in the book, in his life) Eiseley will return to this trope until, at last, Eiseley will walk "like a ghost back into the past" to understand this wintry episode. What *are* the facts about these prisoners and their murderous escape? Why does the tale of a convict named Tom Murry continue to haunt him? What has happened to the years? Eiseley reads the now-microfilmed coverage of the escape. He drives to the place where the event took place. Time collapses until it isn't just now and then that are conflated, but also Eiseley and the convict Murry. It's all one moment. It's the brain playing tricks. It's the past as the place we all begin.

First memories are made not from the gloss of things, the one-day-just-like-another, the automaton response to life and its necessities. First memories are activated by some breed of shock to the system, some differentiating cause and effect, some Technicolor confusion or vivid confrontation between the norm and the new. First memories are a first awakening—emblematic, symbolic, telling. First memories are like DNA—as integral to the who of us as our green eyes and auburn hair.

But also this: What we recall about then, what we are capable of knowing about our childhood selves, how we tell ourselves the stories, how we tell them to others—this is all part and parcel of, inextricable from, who we are right now, how we filter the world, how we (again) *value* it. My first memory is about the terrifying insistence of empathy, and a corresponding sense of powerlessness. Canetti's first memory is about fear, perhaps, but mostly about its tantalizations. Moses's first memory is about stolen sweets and the need to possess such deliciousness. Ansay's first memory is about the fear of forgetting, which is also the fear of losing, which is of course a pivotal life theme for a woman from whom mobility, not to mention piano song, will be taken.

Your first memory may not be the beginning of your memoir; certainly the story I just told about those purloined streamers does not stand at the beginning of any of my books. Your second, third, or fourth memories may not factor in, either, but that's all right. We're still a few pages away from our actual book work—still working, here, with raw material. So write your first memory, and then your second, and then your third, and after your pages are filled and your arm is aching, look back over the stories that you have called up, revealed. Look for the consistencies, story to story. Consider what they reveal about you. What are the half-buried themes, and what are the overt declarations? Do you know yourself better for having tramped around in the past?

In his memoir, *Speak, Memory*, Vladimir Nabokov wrote

this: "In probing my childhood (which is the next best thing to probing one's eternity) I see the awakening of consciousness as a series of spaced flashes, with the intervals between them gradually diminishing until bright blocks of perception are formed, affording memory a slippery hold."

I like that phrase "bright blocks of perception."

I like "probing one's eternity" even better.

REMAIN VULNERABLE

I had never campaigned to teach at the University of Pennsylvania. It took me weeks, after the invitation arrived, to finally say yes. I was worried, first, about time: I run a business, I write books, I am a mother and a wife. I was worried, second, about yield. Did I know enough, had I learned enough, to be the teacher I would expect myself to be?

I had, it was true, been teaching all along—children and teens, midcareer adults and retirees. I'd traveled to universities and talked, joined the faculty of summer programs, mentored high school students, conducted workshops against the backdrop of gladioli and streams, taken on the mantle of writer-in-residence.

But to teach on an Ivy League campus for an entire semester is a different calling altogether. It is a marathon, a form of politics, a performance, and a contest of both popularity and wills. Students are, inevitably, in the know about which teachers are easily managed and which are hardly worth the maneuvers, which show up because they *want* to teach and which because teaching is, finally, a job. A new name on a faculty roster will be evaluated primarily by her one hung shingle: the course description. I worked on mine for weeks, read it to my husband as if it were a poem:

> "Maybe the best we can do is try to leave ourselves unprotected . . ." the poet-novelist Forrest Gander has written. "To approach each other and the world with as much vulnerability as we can possibly sustain." In this advanced nonfiction workshop, we will seek, and leverage, exposure. We'll be reading writers contemplating writing—Natalia Ginzburg, Larry Woiwode, Vivian Gornick, Terrence Des Pres, Annie Dillard. We'll be reading writers writing their own lives—Gretel Ehrlich, Anthony Doerr, Stanley Kunitz, Brooks Hansen, Jean-Dominique Bauby—as well as writers writing the lives of others—Frederick Busch on Terrence Des Pres, for example, Patricia Hampl on her parents, Michael Ondaatje on the utterly cinematic characters of his childhood. The point will be to get close to the bone of things.

"Sounds like an acquired taste," my husband said. (I put this in quotes. It is a fact. He said it.)

Acquired taste. I wavered, then went forward—an ungainly mix of recklessness and abject fear. Can you, in fact, teach vulnerability? Is that where memoir starts?

Semesters have since gone by. Students have entered my life and stayed. My family is big, and it is growing. And I can say now, with confidence: Leave yourself unprotected. Remain vulnerable. For this is where memoir begins.

I've written more than seventeen books in a half-dozen genres since I published my first memoir in 1998. I have written at least one blog post a day since that first intrepid post back in 2007. I say these things not to gloatingly quantify (perhaps I should be embarrassed; some say I should be ashamed) but to make this point: I still only write when the yearning is urgent. I'm dead-in-the-water boring otherwise. And so, of course, is my writing. I yearn a lot, I'm sorry to say. And so I'm always writing.

Urgency is born of vulnerability. Vulnerability makes room for surprise. Surprise must be exercised; it is a state of mind. You didn't see that coming? Good. You can't believe you cried? Thank God you're human. Beauty blazes through you, beauty makes you feel alive, you can't sleep sometimes because of beauty's ten-fingered grip, because of the shattering glory of the evening sky? It's all right. We insomniacs get you. You've wondered sometimes whether it's true that souls don't bleed, because you're pretty sure your soul has bled when you hugged your students good-bye, and when your son graduated, and when somebody played your mother's song and you couldn't turn to her and smile? You've wondered? I've wondered, too. The questions, the feelings, the hurt, the awe, the beguilement come at me, and because I have remained vulnerable, because I don't even know how to buckle the armor or shine the shield, I am affected (call it afflicted) and I see story.

I use music and movement to maintain this state of mind—taking long walks before I write to shake my muscles loose, to knock the ache out of my joints, to stretch, and then to see. Down the hill, past the church, around the bend, and *bam*, there it is—the blue rope of a thin snake in the street, or the wide shell of a horny tortoise, or a briny-backed deer in the woods, or a marigold, or perhaps my friend Kathleen, eighty years old, here with a story about the circus. There's not an entire memoir in this; I wouldn't suggest the preposterous. But what there is—what I need—is that tremble or curiosity or déjà vu that sets a memory free.

Or maybe it's raining and I have the house to myself. Maybe I don't care if I never did buy curtains and any enterprising neighbor could see. I play Bruce Springsteen until the house is shaking—his river songs, his glory ballads. I play him until I have him in the hollow of my bones, until it is not my true self in the reflecting window glass but a phantom version—a ghostly, smoky mystery. Vulnerable? Yes. Cracked open, anticipating? That, too.

Always I make sure that, even as I teach, I don't neglect my role—my privilege—as a student of so many things. As a student of cultures, when I travel. As a student of photography. As a student of gardens or a student of rivers, or a student of the rumba, samba, waltz. I'll go to a studio and I'll submit to the instructions of a real dancer half my age. He'll tell me that I don't stand straight or that I don't let the music steep or that I have to stop fighting myself to master the *swoosh* or the contagious quicks of the cha-cha. He will say, Do not be ashamed by your insatiable wanting, or your need for lyric and lift. Do not be ashamed. Dance it.

Our best teachers teach us more about life than about anything else. They give us the chance to be slightly better people. They listen to us so that we can start listening to ourselves, so that we can remove all the junk that lies between us and our own authority, our own capacity for remembering. It doesn't matter who you are or what you do: Don't lose your urgency. Don't yield to the suspicion that you know enough, have seen enough, have wanted enough, have danced the perfect rumba. Don't get yourself all pretty, perfect, and complete. Value imbalance. Remain vulnerable.

THREE

GET MOVING

WHAT'S IT ALL ABOUT?

YOUR memoir must negate chronology with wisdom, presumption with knowing, misty maybes with a more robust version of life as it was lived.

Do you know, yet, what you're writing about?

Do you know what is at stake?

Do you know what questions and hopes, suggestions and pervasions will ride like a sine curve behind your prose— sometimes overt, sometimes subtle, always implicating?

There are no right or wrong answers here. There is no instantaneous knowing. There is only the requirement that you think these matters through. Memoirists work like gardeners in spring—planting the seeds, clearing the weeds, harvesting the bright-headed crop, arranging the stems. Memoirists must be patient—not just with themselves but also with the mass of material, and with the impulse to tell. Memoirists must understand, as well, what it is, exactly, that has propelled them into this land of terrible beauty and great danger.

In a letter to Willa Cather, Sarah Orne Jewett suggests that what "belongs to Literature" is the stuff born of a long, nagging itch: "The thing that teases the mind over and over for years, and at last gets itself put down rightly on paper—whether little or great, it belongs to Literature." Terrence Des Pres (channeling Henry James) suggests in *Writing into the World*, that we have little choice in the writing matter: "What we select to write about . . . isn't a matter of choice so much as being chosen. Writing of every kind begins, as Henry James said, with its *donnée*, the something given, the one small thing that cannot be refused."

Memoir is active, it is alert, it is not lazy. It is about asking the right questions about the past and about the human condition. What leads to violence? What is the aftermath of abrasion? How does one survive loss? Why do we tell ourselves stories to protect ourselves from the chaos of experience? How are big things small and small things big? How do the refrains from the past shape the reality of our present? Who the hell was I? What was I thinking? And if it happened to me, does it happen to you? How does *my* story get me closer to *us*?

Sometimes you can get at those questions obliquely, through structure and white space. Sometimes you do it by rubbing the now against the then. Sometimes we accentuate the terrible discrepancy. Sometimes you are writing toward forgiveness—of yourself, of others. This is the beauty of memoir. If all your memoir does is deliver story—no sediments, no tidewater, no ambiguity—readers have no reason to return. If you cannot embrace the messy tug of yourself, the inescapable contradictions, the ugly and the lovely, then you are not ready yet. If you can't make room for us, then please don't expect us to start making room for you.

Kim, my dark-haired student with the Cleopatra eyes,

chose to write her memoir about luckiness, unluckiness, and love. My favorite paragraph:

> Love makes you dependent; pain pushes you to the breaking point of self-actualization. My parents' support and the stability they provided for me is something I'm still trying to justify by replacing their hands with my own, finger by finger. Every day I lift a barricade to get through hermitage and extroversion, harmony and entropy, my mother's love and my mother's illness, innovation and inundation. I was lucky, I was born an American, I was born healthy, I was born into a loving home. I was unlucky, I was born judgmental, I have seen terror, I have seen desperate cries for life. So we continue: surprised, derisive, and awake by intuition.

Jonathan wrote about prayer as hobby, and about religious fanaticism:

> Prayer was my new hobby, easily eating up an hour of every morning. My religious observance became systematic: I had to make sure experimental conditions were optimal. Experiments fail if they aren't perfectly calibrated—perhaps my prayer was similarly ineffective because I was ignoring some ritualistic detail. Scientific precision was giving way to religious fanaticism. I was too skeptical of reality to reject superstition so quickly—and I had so much to lose. For two years, I was blinded by minutiae. Then I found academic biblical analysis.

Gabe wrote about surviving a heart condition; more than that, though, he wrote to imagine what a son's illness means to a mother:

> This was also probably what she begged for when, after I had gone unconscious in the hospital that day in February, the doctor spoke with her and told her that her son was very sick and that every effort was being made to save him. She had flown to Peru the night before to be with her father who was on his deathbed. She must have hung up the phone, heard the echo of the handset hitting the cradle resounding in her head, and felt her knees buckling beneath her. She somehow gathered strength, said what she thought was a last goodbye to her dying father, and boarded a plane towards Philadelphia. Those eight hours of flight must have been claustrophobically helpless. No jet plane could have flown fast enough to make this trip bearably short. No altitude could have brought her close enough to God so that she could scream loud enough in his ear to please save her son.

Responsibility—to one's self and to others—was the theme that engaged Stephanie.

> How much of your life, the life you know, is actually your own? We all do things for others, stretching out limbs like a thigmotropic plant clinging to the structure of another to both give and receive life-sustaining supplements. But what do we do for

ourselves that we do not do for others? What moments are we robbed of, what people do we give
too much to? And when, if ever, are we truly
independent?

No one can or should tell you what to write about. But
if you don't know where the memoir impulse is coming
from, if you can't trace it, can't defend it, can't articulate an
answer when somebody asks "Why'd you want to write a
memoir anyway?"—stop. Hold those memoir horses. Either
the mind has been teased for years upon years, or there's that
small thing that won't be refused, or there's something else
genuine and worthy. But nobody wants to hear that you're
writing memoir because you need some quick cash, or because you think it will make you famous, or because your
boyfriend said there's a movie in this, or because you're just
so mad and it's about time you get to tell your version.

So know why you're writing, and then know this: No
memoir in the history of memoirs has ever written itself.
Every recorded story, detail, metaphor, and pause repre-
sents a decision made. You will be writing a life story that
leaves (by necessity) the vast majority of your life story off
the page. You will use these elisions to your advantage,
elevate details into symbols, find the heart of a story within
the fringe of a vignette, shuffle the chapters of time in
search of answers. You will remain vulnerable and tell the
truth and still, somehow, make certain that the story you
tell is yours to tell and not a violation of trust. You will
get there.

But at first you're going to need to wallow around in
early drafts. You're going to need to experiment. Write the

you in present tense, the you in past tense, the landscape, the weather, the song, the color of your life, the self-analysis. Buy several notebooks. Suppress no urge, douse no flame, do not be shy. These are drafts, and when you draft, you keep your self-censor in the closet.

You'll know when you're ready. You'll know when it's time to turn and face the book. Time to define your frames and filters, identify your themes, and conscientiously—and artfully—proclaim (to yourself only, at first): My memoir is about navigating loss. My memoir is about second chances. My memoir is about the power of love. My memoir is about injustice overcome. My memoir is about coming to terms with middle age. My memoir is about foreignness. My memoir is about defining home. My memoir is about the power of the imagination.

All of which is not quite what the pseudo-memoirists say. My memoir is about the time my sister rode across the country on a horse and left me behind with a pitchfork, says the pseudo. My memoir is about how I had to work so hard so that my wife could stay home and whittle. My memoir is about the second aunt on my stepsister's side who ate green-pea soup every day, for lunch and also supper. My memoir is about a house I built. My memoir is about a fishing trip. My memoir is about how much I hate my mother. The pseudos haven't climbed out of their own small circles yet. The pseudos haven't connected with the larger world, or with their readers. The pseudos are confusing anecdote with memoir. The pseudos collect the critics' ire. They mess it up for the rest of us.

The pseudos just clearly aren't ready yet. They need more time with the material. They need to more profoundly *know*. It's not that we don't want their details, or the recipe for that green-pea soup, or a vivid image of that crafty wife's best whittling job. It's that we need to know what it all *means*, and how it relates to us. Simple truths. It's just not memoir without them.

"A memoir is a work of sustained narrative prose controlled by an idea of the self under obligation to lift from the raw material of life a tale that will shape experience, transform event, deliver wisdom," Vivian Gornick writes in her essential guide, *The Situation and the Story*. "Truth in a memoir is achieved not through a recital of actual events; it is achieved when the reader comes to believe that the writer is working hard to engage with the experience at hand. What happened to the writer is not what matters; what matters is the large sense that the writer is able to *make* of what happened. For that the power of a writing imagination is required. As V. S. Pritchett once said of the genre, 'It's all in the art. You get no credit for living.'"

In *The Art of Time in Memoir*, Sven Birkerts speaks not about engaging experience but about redeeming it. He speaks of patterns. He speaks of memoir as having the power not just to showcase but also to explain: "The memoirist writes, above all else, to redeem experience, to re-awaken the past, and to find its pattern; better yet, he writes to discover behind bygone events a dramatic explanatory narrative."

And if you're not yet convinced, read (I implore you) Patricia Hampl, especially "Memory and Imagination," which appears in the essay collection *I Could Tell You Stories*. I have never taught a memoir class without assigning these sweet, instructive seventeen pages. I never go far, and no memoirist should go far, without thinking of Hampl's words, quoted earlier: "True memoir is written, like all of literature, in an attempt to find not only a self but a world."

What world do you live in? And how will you bridge your world to mine? And what will you say when somebody asks you: *What is your memoir about?*

BEGINNINGS

ENOUGH. You've got your question(s). You suspect your themes. You've got ideas about frame or, at the very least, a willingness to search for one. You've worked your voice onto the page in a way that sounds like you. You've got notebooks full of scenes and stories. The memoir must begin.

The memoir needs a beginning.

Beginnings, clearly, set the tone. They extend an invitation, issue a warning, throw down a bridge. They let readers know what might be at stake. They foreshadow a book's relative complications, making it clear, from the start, whether the story will be complex or direct, tangled or straight-shooting. Beginnings signal the quality of the author's voice—how trustworthy, how revealing, how descriptive, how matter-of-fact, how dependent on the actual or the imagined. Beginnings tell the reader in the bookstore; the reader with an iPad, a Nook, a Kindle; the reader at a book club meeting whether or not he will want to read more. And before any of that, beginnings declare a project's market value to agents and editors. (I hate to be crass, but there it is.)

Not always but often, memoirists introduce themselves to readers with a prologue. Think of the prologue as a buffer zone, as an easing toward, as prefatory. Consider all the room it offers to suggest theme and tone and frame, the percolating entanglements of the memoir's story lines. Consider how efficiently it can establish mood.

I advocate prologue in memoir. I find that it helps everyone involved—the writer, the reader—if certain early declarations are made. The thrill of literary memoir isn't bound up in plot, per se, and it shouldn't be bound up in gossip. The thrill of the genre—or, at least, one of its chief pleasures—is all webbed into just how well the author manages to answer the questions or explore the themes or concerns that lie at the story's heart. Coy doesn't work—or at least I don't think it does. The questions, themes, and concerns that fuel a memoir are often best enunciated at the start. And prologues (call these opening zones prefaces, if you like) are such fine, flexible containers. You can make them do whatever you want them to do. You can even give them different names.

Some examples. In *Into the Tangle of Friendship: A Memoir of the Things That Matter*, my second book, I was interested in understanding how the people who enter our lives shape who we become. I begin with a scene, but embedded in that scene are the questions that will rise and fall throughout the ensuing narrative:

Call the wooden climber in the center the seat of power. Call the sandbox and the swings and the splintered tables the hearts of commerce; the shade beneath the oaks, the church; the ravaged muddy creek beyond, this country's borderlands. It is spring—a puckering day. The kids—alone, in pairs, afraid, delighted, in cars, on foot, in a parade of rusty wagons, on the verge of brave entanglements— have finally come.

Out on the playground's edge, the sun at my back, I sit and wait and wonder. I watch. I know that the coming hours will shape the children's view of friendship and, consequently, their view of themselves. I know that there will be struggles, winners, losers, so many one-act plays, mysteries and parables. Who is the leader here, and who the disciple? Who will betray, who can be trusted? Who will be drawn in, who locked out? How will passions coalesce, what will be talked about, who will care? When will the accretion of events, hopes, revelations, gifts, become the stuff of memory and faith, a durable philosophy of friendship?

[A few pages later] . . . What do any of us know about friendship, isn't that the question here? What can we make of how it changes over time, how it is about wonder at first, then self-definition, then survival, how it is always about comfort, about simply being here, alive? How do we come to terms with the responsibilities and limitations, the possibility of schisms and despair? Because isn't it true that the more we let others into our lives, the safer we become and also the more endangered. Isn't it worth it nonetheless? Friendships matter; they rebut death, they tie us to this earth, and, when we're gone, they keep us here; our friends remember us.

Looking back and looking forward we see that this is true: friendship stands as both a scaffolding and a bridge.

In *Seeing Past Z: Nurturing the Imagination in a Fast-Forward World*, I don't call the prologue "Prologue." I call it "Imagining Tomorrow." It ends with these words:

I want to raise my son to pursue wisdom over winning. I want him to channel his passions and talents and personal politics into rivers of his choosing. I'd like to take the chance that I feel it is my right to take on contentment over credentials, imagination over conquest, the idiosyncratic point of view over the standard-issue one. I'd like to live in a world where that's okay.

Some call this folly. Some make a point of reminding me of all the most relevant data: That the imagination has lost its standing in classrooms and families nationwide. That storytelling is for those with too much time. That winning early is one bet-hedging path toward winning later on. That there isn't time, as there once was time, for a child's inner life. That a mother who eschews competition for conversation is a mother who places her son at risk for second-class citizenry.

Perhaps. But I have this boy with these two huge dark eyes who thinks and plays and speculates. I have a boy who is emergent and hopeful, intuitive and funny, somewhere between childhood and adolescence. How will he define himself as the years unfold? What will he claim as his own? What will he craft of the past? What will he do with what he thinks, make of what he dreams, invent out of the stuff of all his passions? It is my right—it is my obligation, even—to sit with him for a while longer, imagining tomorrow.

I don't mean to sound extreme. Not every memoir prologue serves as the great question reveal; they don't all rely on the snaking question mark. Frank Conroy's classic memoir, *Stop-Time*, a book about childhood and adolescence, begins with a page torn out of Conroy's adult life. It's a terrifying four paragraphs—that's it—about Conroy's trips to London "once or twice a week in a wild, escalating passion of frustration, blinded by some mysterious mixture of guilt, moroseness, and desire." Conroy doesn't pose his question outright. He doesn't even feel compelled to make the direct connection between those wild adult nights and the childhood story to come. We understand, implicitly, that who Conroy became is a function of who he was, and who his childhood allowed him to be. We have been introduced. And now we read.

Lucy Grealy, in *Autobiography of a Face*, uses her prologue to tell a story about pony parties, to invite us in. "My friend Stephen and I used to do pony parties together," the book begins, and so with a sideways glance, with winning innocence, Grealy announces what she's up to here. She is not writing a story about her childhood cancer and its devastating effects to win our sympathy. No, indeed, she's going to keep that cancer at bay for as long as she can. She's going to write about beauty, its absence, a child's wisdom, an adolescent's struggle, the futility all of us feel, at times, about fitting in. To what? To whose standards? To what end result? Her prologue prepares us for the force of her intelligence.

In *Hiroshima in the Morning*, a memoir about, among other things, the consequences of forgetting and the dangers of solitude, Rahna Reiko Rizzuto uses her prologue to issue a warning: "I can tell you the story but it won't be true," she begins. "It won't be the facts as they happened exactly, each day, each footstep, each breath. Time elides, events shift; sometimes we shift them on purpose and forget that we did. Memory is just how we choose to remember." Those who wade into Rizzuto's memoiristic waters know at once what they are in for. An impressionistic book. A shift-and-slide book. A search, not a gung-ho plot.

In *Blue Nights*, a memoir about regrets, aging, a daughter's dying, Joan Didion gives us color as mood: "In certain latitudes there comes a span of time approaching and following the summer solstice, some weeks in all, when the twilights turn long and blue." Blue will sustain this heartbreaking narrative. Blue draws its curtains around it.

With *The Tender Bar*, J. R. Moehringer gives us a choral *we* in a prologue that introduces his tale about being raised among tall drafts and beer talk, and in the absence of the person who was supposed to love him most. Everything to come, in this memoir, is here, in this first paragraph—sometimes explicit, sometimes metaphoric. We know, thanks to the prologue, just what we're in for.

We went there for everything we needed. We went there when thirsty, of course, and when hungry, and when dead tired. We went there when happy, to celebrate, and when sad, to sulk. We went there after weddings and funerals, for something to settle our nerves, and always for a shot of courage just before. We went there when we didn't know what we needed, hoping someone might tell us. We went there when looking for love, or sex, or trouble, or for someone who had gone missing, because sooner or later everyone turned up there. Most of all we went there when we needed to be found.

In her glorious memoir about her friendship with Robert Mapplethorpe, *Just Kids*, Patti Smith uses her opening pages (she titles them "Foreword") to walk us into her frame. This will be, it's clear, the story of a best friend vanished. This will be a meditation—the things that were set against the things that disappeared. This will be an accounting of a relationship that was always tipped toward imbalance. This will not be a judgment; it will be a blessing.

I was asleep when he died. I had called the hospital to say one more good night, but he had gone under, beneath layers of morphine. I held the receiver and listened to his labored breathing through the phone, knowing I would never hear him again.

Later I quietly straightened my things, my notebook and fountain pen. The cobalt inkwell that had been his. My Persian cup, my purple heart, a tray of baby teeth. I slowly ascended the stairs, counting them, fourteen of them, one after another.

I drew the blanket over the baby in her crib, kissed my son as he slept, then lay down beside my husband and said my prayers. He is still alive, I remember whispering. Then I slept.

Here's how Meghan O'Rourke prepares us for her journey through loss—with a story stolen from childhood about a town on the banks of the Battenkill, a dog named Finn, and the mother O'Rourke will lose too young. Loss is open-ended. It cannot finally be reconciled. It leaves us bewildered. It leaves us yearning. The final paragraph from the lilting prologue to *The Long Goodbye* is palpable with ache and desire:

When we are learning the world, we know things we cannot say how we know. When we are re-learning the world in the aftermath of a loss, we feel things we had almost forgotten, old things, beneath the seat of reason. These memories in me of my mother are almost as deep as the memories that led Finn to flush and point. As the fireflies began to rise one summer evening, my mother called to us. *Look*, she said. *See them? Run and get a jar and a can opener.* And my brother and I ran in for jars and our mother poked holes in the lids and sent us across the lawn to catch the fireflies. The air was the temperature of our skin.

With his prologue to *No Heroes*, a memoir recounting his return to the hills of Kentucky, Chris Offutt establishes his outsiderliness from the very start. He tells you the facts—he's been gone twenty years—and he tells you how hard this chapter in his life is going to be. Offutt uses his prologue to put us on his side, to prepare us for all we will see. He asks the question, without employing the question mark, of whether any of us can really go back home again.

No matter how you leave the hills—the army, prison, marriage, a job—when you move back after twenty years, the whole country is carefully watching. They want to see the changes that the outside world put on you. They are curious to know if you've lost your laughter. They are worried that perhaps you've gotten above your raisings.

To reassure the community, you should dress down except when you have to dress up, then wear your Sunday-go-to-meeting clothes. Make sure you drive a rusty pickup truck that runs like a sewing machine, flies low on the straight stretch, and hauls block up a creek bed. Hang dice from the mirror and a gun rack in the back window. A rifle isn't necessary, but something needs to be there—a pool cue, a carpenter's level, an ax handle. Where the front plate should be, screw one on that says "American by birth, Kentuckian by the grace of God."

Finally, consider the power of italics on a first, untitled page. Consider, in other words, what Michael Ondaatje does at the very start of *Running in the Family*, a memoir built from fragments. Ondaatje is, with these opening lines, telegraphing his process, acknowledging the truth that recollecting childhood is hard and dangerous work. It will steal your dreams. It will unwrap time. It will not come easily, and the story will tumble, and for a while, at least, the boy that Ondaatje was will appear as a character, not just to us but also to him. Ondaatje doesn't need to name his prologue and, indeed, had the word appeared on the page it would have interfered with the organic quality of the prose. But this is prologue as poetry, prologue as song, prologue as the writer working near.

> *Drought since December.*
>
> *All across the city men roll carts with ice clothed in sawdust. Later on, during a fever, the drought still continuing, his nightmare is that thorn trees in the garden send their hard roots underground towards the house climbing through windows so they can drink the sweat off his body, steal the last of the saliva off his tongue.*
>
> *He snaps on the electricity just before daybreak. For twenty-five years he has not lived in this country, though up to the age of eleven he slept in rooms like this—with no curtains, just delicate bars across the windows so no one could break in. And the floors of red cement polished smooth, cool against bare feet.*
>
> *Dawn through a garden. Clarity to leaves, fruit, the dark yellow of the King Coconut. This delicate light is allowed only a brief moment of the day. In ten minutes the garden will lie in a blaze of heat, frantic with noise and butterflies.*
>
> *Half a page—and the morning is already ancient.*

Again: Maybe you'll decide to write a prologue (or a preface or an untitled italicized block) for your memoir.

Maybe you won't. It is far from mandatory. What *is* mandatory is that you spend real time thinking about and working with your beginning. Don't cop to mere chronology, unless chronology is a theme or a question. Don't merely explain; this isn't journalism. Don't simply plunge in, assuming we'll follow along; we're only following, I can promise you this, if you've been smart and deliberate about your proximities and patterns, the nearness and farness of your voice. If all I wanted was to know what happened to some stranger from earliest memory through most recent, I'd be reading autobiography. As far as I can tell, you're signing up for memoir here. Write considered first lines, provocative first lines, telling first lines, self-disclosing first lines, first lines that hold the entire book within themselves, like a seed.

Draw us in. Seduce us.

BLANK PAGE

THAT'S right. That's what I have for you here. A blank page.

It's all yours.

Use it.

Perhaps you'll write your entire first draft in one fell swoop—your boyfriend bringing you cups of tea, your cat curling around your legs, your phone ringing incessant and unanswered, your Twitter feed silent. Perhaps you will take pieces of things, the fragments you've been writing all along—your weather, your color, your mother's kitchen— and lay them out on a narrow table, one beside the other, until the right interrelationships reveal themselves and prompt the story. Perhaps it's just one line that you have so far—one line, but it's a good one. Perhaps you'll work like an architect of old, laying sheets of trace paper above your typed prose to find the bend in time.

Perhaps.

FOUR

FAKE NOT AND
OTHER LAST WORDS

FAKE NOT

TO write memoir is to enter, as we have seen, a war zone—with yourself, with the ones you love, with the critics you may never meet. It is to lay your life on a line, on several lines. You may be ridiculed, harassed, taken down in the court of public opinion. Worse, your aunt Mathilda may never speak to you again. You may be called upon to defend the form. You may feel the need. Your sole protection will be the work itself—its integrity, its artfulness, its originality, its capacity to entertain or seduce, its implicit recognition that you are not, in the end, the only person who ever had a story to tell, the only person worth listening to. What you are, if you're a memoirist, is a person who has been trusted to help us see, or help us think, or remind us that we (the rest of all us *mes*) are not alone.

Think you're ready? Feel immune? Have you coffee'd lately with Neil Genzlinger who, writing in the *New York Times Book Review*, revealed that he had just communed with the memoir listings on Amazon? Tens of thousands of titles, he reported, and the small minority of "memoir-eligible" authors were, in his words:

. . . lost in a sea of people you've never heard of, writing uninterestingly about the unexceptional, apparently not realizing how commonplace their little wrinkle is or how many other people have already written about it. Memoirs have been disgorged by virtually everyone who has ever had cancer, been anorexic, battled depression, lost weight. By anyone who has ever taught an underprivileged child, adopted an underprivileged child or been an underprivileged child. By anyone who was raised in the '60s, '70s or '80s, not to mention the '50s, '40s or '30s. Owned a dog. Run a marathon. Found religion. Held a job.

Genzlinger is just one voice in a choral crowd that has had it with, in his words, this "absurdly bloated genre." I've introduced you, already, to others. Perhaps you have started to marvel at my moxie and devotion—because I not only write and teach memoir; I also am *writing* about writing and teaching memoir. Marvel on, I say. I'm used to that. I can spot a raised eyebrow a mile away.

There are those who suggest—overtly and otherwise— that the cure for memoir is the redefining, or perhaps undefining, of memoir. Let it lie a little more. Let it extravagantly cheat. Allow it to let down its tangled, rootsy hair. *Wink. Wink.* Give it more room. Absolute, uncontested, thoroughly documented truth, we've established, is impossible when the primary source or instigator is a fickle brain. And so there will be gaps; why not just fill them? And so there will be interpretations; why not just claim? We lie by omission. We lie by trying to be kind. We lie because we love.

We lie because we hate. We lie because we're ashamed. What does memoir think it is, anyway? We're all just tumbling around here on Planet Earth. Who *can* handle the truth?

If we can't remember everything, if our memories change every time we recall them, if our brother is sure (he'll bet you the house) that your blue is his pink, your river his stream, if Ben Yagoda thinks we're mostly self-promoting liars, if Neil Genzlinger is pretty close to certain that he's read your memoir before, at least twice since last Sunday, shouldn't we pull our chair up to another literary feast? Sign up for a different genre team? Declare our methodology in a manner that gives the work that follows meaning?

Many writers do. Take *A Heartbreaking Work of Staggering Genius* from your shelf, and read Dave Eggers's preface: "For all the author's bluster elsewhere, this is not, actually, a work of pure nonfiction. Many parts have been fictionalized in varying degrees, for various purposes." Eggers informs us that the dialogue has "of course been almost entirely reconstructed." He tells us that the author, meaning himself, "had to change a few names, and further disguise these named-changed characters." He tells us that "there have been a few instances of location-switching." And he fesses up to omissions: "Some really great sex scenes were omitted, at the request of those who are now married or involved."

Eggers tells us what we're in for, in other words. He grasses up his fearless, fearsome playing field. You're going to like this, or you won't. You're going to play along or, if it's memoir you're seeking, you're going to find another book. However you, the reader, responds, Eggers, the writer, has been truthful. He has not led you blind into a false confessional.

By his own accounting, Eggers has not written unadulterated *memoir*. Neither has the self-proclaimed Bloggess, Jenny Lawson, who gives her memoir—*Let's Pretend This Never Happened*—a leeway-liberating subtitle: *A Mostly True Memoir*.

All right. Wink.

But many writers offering steep disclaimers still shelf their books among nonfiction, a choice that puzzles me. *Reading Lolita in Tehran* is, of course, an important book in so many ways, recounting as it does the two years the author gathered Iranian women in her home to read and share Western literature. This is a book with something to say, something to teach, something to reveal. But look at Azar Nafisi's author's note, which I reproduce in its entirety:

Aspects of characters and events in this story have been changed mainly to protect individuals, not just from the eye of the censor but also from those who read such narratives to discover who's who and who did what to whom, thriving on and filling their own emptiness through others' secrets. The facts of this story are true insofar as any memory is ever truthful, but I have made every effort to protect friends and students, baptizing them with new names and disguising them perhaps even from themselves, changing and interchanging facets of their lives so that their secrets are safe.

Now consider the description below, found early in the book. Beautifully written, of course. Evocative, absolutely. But because we have been warned that names and features and personal histories have all been thoroughly squished together and remixed, it's difficult to know what to do with these "facts." If these personal details—so lovingly drawn, so particular—aren't true, what else is? Or perhaps some of it *is* true, but how are we to know? What should guide us?

> Mahshid is proper in the true sense of the word: she has grace and a certain dignity. Her skin is the color of moonlight, and she has almond-shaped eyes and jet-black hair. She wears pastel colors and is soft-spoken. Her pious background should have shielded her, but it didn't. I cannot imagine her in jail.
>
> Over the many years I have known Mahshid, she has rarely alluded to her jail experiences, which left her with a permanently impaired kidney. . . .

Many secrets must be protected. Many people should be kept hidden from prying eyes. But when so much fictionalizing goes into making a book, it is no longer memoir. If you're changing all the names on purpose, if you're writing what might have been, if deliberate disguise is your method, if you are leaning hard on half truths, if your memoir feels like so much fiction *even to you*, it's time to take your story—your still valid, still potent story—and set it free in another genre. Because nonfiction, as Sallie Tisdale has written, "is supposed to tell the truth—and telling the truth is what people *suppose* us to do."

Don't ruin memoir for the rest of us. Don't discourage and unsettle us. Don't join James Frey (*A Million Little Pieces*) and Margaret Seltzer (*Love and Consequences*) and all the obvious scammers. You'll leave us feeling culpable for your lies, for buying into them. Or you'll leave *me* feeling that way.

Here, from my personal treasure trove of shame, is an example: One cold rainy winter day, I carried a book I was reading to a friend of mine. I sat in his office and read it out loud. Said, through my teary, cracked green eyes: *Listen to the beauty of this*. I talked about the power of the book. I talked about the importance of the story. I talked about the talents of the author. I took my friend's *time*, intoning as I turned the pages of the book:

I want to tell you about my son. That is why I am writing all this down in some mad, frenetic attempt to share him with you.

If I do *nothing* else with what is left of my life, let me do this. Let me show you something extraordinarily unique, something more beautiful than *anything* you have ever seen. Something mad. Mad to live.

Inside a dream.

The story of Awee if very much like the story of Awee running bases.

You know he's going to make it home, but you hold your breath as he slides through the human obstacles that stand directly in his way.

I could take his picture. He's standing there with his teammates. Their arms draped around him because they love him. But it really wouldn't tell you much about who Awee is.

. . .

Awee was eleven years old when he came to me. Adopted.

This *entire* book (and then some) could be about his eyes.

I didn't find out until some time later that the memoir I'd read with such dramatic passion—*The Boy and the Dog Are Sleeping*, which was acclaimed, by the way, which was award-winning—was a hoax. Its author, who had christened himself Nasdijj and had claimed to have been raised on a Navajo reservation by a white cowboy and a Navajo mother, was in fact Tim Barrus, a white man, a writer of gay erotica, a borrower of other people's styles and stories, a man who would soon become famously angry at any attempt to uncover his proxy.

It doesn't matter that I wasn't the only one duped by Tim Barrus—the prize givers, the gushing reviewers, the enthusing early readers stood right there with me. I still feel shame at having been among the believers. I still blush at the fervency of my faith in his story, by how I had been language seduced.

I'd let his language seduce me. I'd been fooled.

It's obvious, right? Don't lie on purpose when writing memoir. Don't appropriate other people's tragedies as your own, or turn yourself into some kind of sexy outlaw, if you are actually not. Don't say you are a half–Native American girl, a foster child even, a drug runner more so, a gang gal (come *on*) if you are white through and through and were raised in a wealthy Los Angeles neighborhood by your own attentive parents. Don't fabricate a boy and make us love him; we'd have loved him just as much (okay, maybe not *as* much, but close) if you'd called him what he was, which was a fiction.

Try, instead, to get as close as possible to the what-actually-was. I have said it; I shall repeat myself; I want to be perfectly clear. We understand that what we remember dislodges and agitates during the very act of remembering. We recognize that the important stuff may lie in the glimmers and shadows, in the imprecisions, in the misremembered. We know that any dialogue that lives outside a transcript is iffy at best. We know that shaping a life means choosing a life means leaving a lot of it out. Memoir requires of us artistry. Sometimes life is anything but.

Still: Best not to pretend we affirmatively know when we don't know at all. Best not to polish up something quasi until it feels like, looks like, maybe could pass for something absolute. "Our lives are uncertain . . ." Sallie Tisdale also said in her pivotal essay, "Violation." "Make that uncertainty part of what you tell."

Take your uncertainty inspiration from, say, *The Liars' Club*. Time and again, Mary Karr confesses that her sister, Lecia, would tell the story differently. Time and again she says one version or another of: *I don't remember this part; it might have gone something like this.* Sometimes Karr goes so far as to share competing tales so that we readers might choose. We love Karr for this. We trust Karr for this. We get it, because we're human, too.

Here's an example, mid-scene. Lecia and Mary are stuffed into the back of their mother's car as she races out of town ahead of a projected killer storm. The mother is Nervous to begin with. She left town far too late. This endangered carload has gotten as far as a very steep bridge, and an accident is waiting to happen. Karr is roping out the scene—keeping it vivid, keeping it alive. That she stops to tell us that her memory isn't precisely what her sister's is does not slow this story down.

> Lecia contends that at this point I started screaming, and that my screaming prompted Mother to wheel around and start grabbing at me, which caused what happened next. (Were Lecia writing this memoir, I would appear in one of only three guises: sobbing hysterically, wetting my pants in a deliberately inconvenient way, or biting somebody, usually her, with no provocation.)
> I don't recall that Mother reached around to grab at me at all. And I flatly deny screaming. But despite my old trick of making my stomach into a rock, I did get carsick.

Do you want another example? Then look at Patti Smith in *Just Kids* and her confession—perfectly understandable, reassuringly human—of hazy early memories. Nothing is lost in the not-quite-remembering. Indeed, the sentences are particulate and lush:

> When I was very young, my mother took me for walks in Humboldt Park, along the edge of the Prairie River. I have vague memories, like impressions on glass plates, of an old boathouse, a circular band shell, an arched stone bridge.

Alice Ozma begins *The Reading Promise: My Father and the Books We Shared* with a declaration, an inviolable-seeming truth: "It started on a train. I am sure of it. The 3,218-night reading marathon that my father and I call The Streak started on a train to Boston, when I was in third grade." We have no reason not to believe Ozma; we're not interested in wrestling with her record. It's Ozma herself who introduces uncertainty—a trust-inducing solution. Turn the page, and it's there:

> If you ask my father, though, as many people recently have, he'll paint an entirely different picture.
>
> "Lovie," he tells me, as I patiently endure his version of the story, "you're cracked in the head. Do you want to know what really happened or are you just going to write down whatever thing comes to mind?"

Orhan Pamuk, writing in *Istanbul*, professes his tendency to exaggerate. There are those, he says, who disagree with his version of things. There is, for him, the leeway he gives himself by focusing not on accuracy but symmetry. I don't agree with Pamuk here about symmetry trumping accuracy. Both can be achieved, and both must. But I trust his account because he's copped to his process. He lets us know which lines to read between.

> Later, when reminded of those brawls, my mother and my brother claimed no recollection of them, saying that, as always, I'd invented them just for the sake of something to write about, just to give

myself a colorful and melodramatic past. They were
so sincere that I was finally forced to agree, con-
cluding that, as always, I'd been swayed more by my
imagination than by real life. So anyone reading
these pages should bear in mind that I am prone to
exaggeration. But what is important for a painter is
not a thing's reality but its shape, and what is important for a novelist is not the course of events but
their ordering, and what is important for a memoirist is not the factual accuracy of the account but its
symmetry.

Finally, consider this from *Half a Life* by Darin Strauss,
who has spent much of his life either running from or trying to re-create the moment when his car hit a girl on a
bike. Most memories aren't continuous. Images come to us
in spurts. We struggle to see; we can't quite see: This, too,
is memoir. Write it down.

This moment has been, for all my life, a kind of
shadowy giant. I'm able, tick by tick, to remember
each second before it. Radio; friends; thoughts of
mini-golf, another thought of maybe just going to
the beach; the distance between the car and bicycle
closing: anything could still happen. But I am
powerless to see what comes next; the moment
raises a shoulder, lowers its head, and slumps away.

I trust Loren Eiseley because of the many times he lets
us know that there are white spaces around his memories,
gaps—and because he does not try to fill them. I trust

Alison Bechdel in her graphic memoir because she leaves evidence of her remembering on the page—her early, confused diary entries; the court report; the images she has drawn not just from memory but also from photographs. I trust Dorothy Allison in *Two or Three Things I Know for Sure* not just because of the photographic record she binds in with her words but also because she issues cautions: "I'm a storyteller. I'll work to make you believe me."

Memoirs are never inferior because memory partially fails or because the journal of record goes suddenly blank or because the raw anecdote must be leavened with some poetry in order to make it psychically true. You are in danger of getting some of it wrong, and I understand, because I am human, too, and because my memory fails me, too, and because trying is the only thing we have, and because I have been wrong, plenty.

Just don't pretend that your story's airtight. Don't write as if there are no other versions. Don't make things up deliberately and hope that I won't notice. Don't assert an inviolable tale. The moment you claim *every word of this is true* is the beginning of my lost faith in you. Take a page from David Carr as you think about your memoir. He tells you all he did to make his story. He tells you why it can't be perfect.

From the author's note for *The Night of the Gun*:

The following book is based on sixty interviews conducted over three years, most of which were recorded on video and/or audio and then transcribed by a third party. The events represented are primarily the product of mutual recollection and discussion. Hundreds of medical files, legal documents, journals, and published reports were used as source material in reconstructing personal history. Every effort was made to corroborate memory with fact and in significant instances where that was not possible, it is noted in the text. . . . All of which is not to say that every word of this book is true—all human stories are subject to errors of omission, fact, or interpretation regardless of intent—only that it is as true as I could make it.

EXERCISE EMPATHY

IT was a Tuesday. I was on my way. My bag was packed—
books, lesson plans, camera. The skies were bright. I locked
the house behind me and hurried past the garden edge,
across the street, toward the old horse show grounds, to
the stone train station. I slid into a window seat after
the train rolled in. I watched the familiar landscape. Teaching is a ritual. The smudged SEPTA-train glass, the backyard views, the occasional cat or opossum, the stray grocery cart, the ballooning plastic bag, the solitary bike
wheel, the hedge of violet-tinted flowers, the fissured
fence, the suburban yielding to the borders of my city—
it's all prelude and segue. I never touch the book on my
lap.

On this particular midmorning, three stops shy of the
Thirtieth Street Station, a kid took the seat next to mine.

"Crowded today," he said.

"Car show at the convention center," I told him.

"All these people for a car show?" he said, turning
around and glancing back at the crowd of white-haired auto
fanatics in the seats behind us. He had a nice face, a clean
profile, Mediterranean skin, this kid. He had a backpack

heavy with books, Penn insignia. We talked about his classes. I told him about mine.

"You write memoir or just teach it?" he asked.

"I've written it," I averred.

"What was it about? Your memoir?"

"Well, that depends," I say, wishing the answer were easier, less list-entailing. "I've written five."

"*Five* memoirs?" The kid seemed startled, genuinely concerned. He felt the need to press. "Isn't five a lot? I mean, how much have you *lived*?"

There are plenty of reasons to write memoir. There are plenty of reasons not to. We've gone through all this. The decision is yours. I have just two more things to ask as you go about handling your truth: Exercise empathy. Seek beauty.

Empathy first, a theme I've touched on, an ideal upon which I would now like to dwell. Because it is that important. Because if you take nothing else from this book, take this. Please.

I'm not going to go all *Merriam-Webster's*. You know what empathy is. You must know why it matters. Not just for the sake of karma, divorce rates, guilt quotients, legal fees, and confession booths but also for the sake of the book—yours. Memoirists who lack empathy produce flat, self-heralding stuff; I hope I've made that clear. They demonstrate no skill for listening, no eye for nuance, no tolerance for opposing points of view. They prove no innate appreciation for the value of complexity or the many-sidedness of the Big Issues. They fail to speak to the ceaseless tug and release, tug and release that lives at the biological, philosophical, and relational heart of life itself. To write without empathy is to drone; it is to lecture; it is to be the only person talking in a crowded room. It is to accuse, and it is, therefore, not memoir.

If the only skin you can imagine is your own, if you cannot walk another's mile, if he is always wrong and you are always right, if it is all your mother's fault, if other people's histories are less important than your own, inhale big time and blow the whistle loud. Go live the weather of a garden. Go skip some stones. Go sift the photographs again. Background. Foreground. What is casting shadows?

Read *The Duke of Deception* (I'm going to have to insist), then ask yourself what good that book would have been had Geoffrey Wolff been writing solely to humiliate or trump his father. Does Wolff pretty up his dad, pretend that things were not terribly hard? Of course not. That would be lying. Does Wolff pretty up himself? No, indeed. He neither lambasts his father nor posits himself as the hero of this heartbreaking childhood tale. Wolff grows up first suspecting, then knowing that his father has fabricated entire swaths of his personal history. He grows up answering to the high expectations of a man who has, in so many ways, failed himself. Writing the memoir affords Wolff the necessary distance—and intimacy—to write passages as deeply steeped in complexity—and humanity—and forgiveness—as this:

> By now I knew my father was a phony. I wasn't dead sure about Yale, but I was sure he was a phony. My father's lesson had taken: he had tried to bring me up valuing precision of language and fact. So around him I became a tyrant of exactitude, not at all what he had meant me to be. Unable to face him down with the gross facts of his

case I nattered at him about details, the *actual* date
of the Battle of Hastings, the world's coldest place,
the distance between the moon and the sun, the
number of vent-holes in a Buick Special. I became
a small-print artist.

I was harder on my father after I had the goods
on him than he had ever been on me. He had always had the goods on me. And he had never made
cruel use of them.

Mira Bartók likewise could have written a thoroughly
condemning account of her schizophrenic artist mother and
had the court of public opinion in her favor. Thankfully, that
wasn't her purpose with *The Memory Palace*. Nor was Bartók
trying to gain her readers' pity as she related the story of the
traumatic car accident that reconfigured the neural pathways
of Bartók's own brain. Bartók's purpose was to contextual-
ize, to understand her mother's compromised brain and, yes,
her bizarre and often hurtful behavior through the lens of
her own injured neurology. The result is measured, quiet—
more questions than answers, not accusation but tender
sadness, a telling decision to quote Nicolaus Steno in the
book: "Beautiful is what we see. More beautiful is what we
understand. Most beautiful if what we do not comprehend."

If Mary Karr had not worked so hard to get to the root
of her mother's Nervous condition, her unsettlingly messy
approach to motherhood, *The Liars' Club* would still be a
Very Good Book. But it would not be the extraordinary
one that it is. We're not interested in jeering at, sneering
over Karr's mother. That's middle school. That's hollow.
We, like Karr, want to know *how* a woman becomes this
troubled, crazed, terrifying, seemingly out-of-touch, but

always somehow near and somehow not not-loving mother. With wit, with poetry, with verve, with suspense, Karr works her way toward an answer.

Dani Shapiro had a difficult relationship with her beautiful mother. That is putting it mildly. Still, look at what Shapiro does toward the end of her memoir, *Devotion*. This is a perilous scene. This is a fearful moment. Shapiro retells it virtuously. She surrenders, to her mother, grace.

The tumors in my mother's brain looked like dust, sprinkled there on the black-and-white lunar landscape of the X-ray. The oncologist pointed to them with the tip of his pencil. "There," he said. "Do you see that? And there." He kept moving his pencil. Finally I began to see that the grayish blur he was showing us was actually dozens—maybe hundreds—of minuscule tumors.

"So how do we get rid of them?" asked my mother.

I sat next to her, close enough to touch. Her winter coat was folded in her lap, and her cane rested against the side of the oncologist's desk. For the first time, my mother looked brittle, as if her bones might break from a fall.

"We don't," the doctor answered. "We can treat them, but . . ." He trailed off, shrugging his shoulders as if to say that these specks were too much for him.

"Mostly, Mrs. Shapiro, what we can do at this point is make you comfortable."

"Comfortable," my mother repeated.

Finally, if Anthony Shadid had, in the course of rebuilding his great-grandfather's estate in Marjayoun, failed
to put all of his difficult interactions with local craftsmen
and construction crews, neighbors and detractors, into empathetic context, *House of Stone* would be a thumbed nose of
a book, an I'm-the-hero-and-they're-the-antagonists stomp
across a war-torn part of the world. But this is Shadid, the
Pulitzer Prize–winning journalist. Shadid, who was known,
in all of his work, not just for his investigative talents, courage, and lyricism but also for his broad-minded compassion.
He puts that to work, over and over, across the pages of his
memoir:

> In Isber's former domain, the ordinary has been,
> for nearly a century, interrupted by war, occupa-
> tion, or what they often call in Arabic "the events."
> These are circumstances that stop time and post-
> pone or conquer living. Traditions die. Everything
> normal is interrupted. Life is not lived in wartime,
> but how long does it take for the breaks in existence
> to be filled? How many generations? This is a na-
> tion in recovery from losses that cannot be remem-
> bered or articulated, but which are everywhere—in
> the head, behind the eyes, in the tears and footsteps
> and words. After life is bent, torn, exploded, there
> are shattered pieces that do not heal for years, if at
> all. What is left are scars and something else—
> shame, I suppose, shame for letting it all continue.
> Glances at the past where solace in tradition and
> myth prevailed only brings more shame over what
> the present is. We have lost the splendors our

ancestors created, and we go elsewhere. People are reminded of that every day here, where an older world, still visible on every corner, fails to hide its superior ways.

Empathy doesn't soften you; it smartens you. Empathy gives you something to say. Empathy stops you—let it stop you—from deliberately hurting those who become essential to the story you feel you must tell.

Your scene centers on a best friend in a hospital, say. How far will you go—*should* you go—in denuding her of her dignity? Are all those intravenous lines, all that blood spurting out of her nose, all that drool, all those excretions the point? Is your story bigger than that? Are you? Are you only writing this down because it feels, well, writerly and shocking to have collected all those details, or because you imagine book club readers exclaiming over your brave and detailed gruesomeness? Are you thinking that you can say what you want because your friend lost her battle with cancer? None of that is reason enough.

A brother appears heartbroken on your doorstep. You're angry at him, sure. You even have every right to be. But how much of his devastation belongs to you? How *broken* must you render him for us to see your point? How, in fact, is he going to feel when he finds your words inside a book that his new girlfriend is also reading? (You never imagined she'd hear about this, you never thought . . .)

Your neighbors are fighting again, hurling insults at each other. It's atmosphere, sure. It says something about the condition, the weather of your own life. It's somehow integral to what you have to say—about suburban life, maybe, or about the permeable quality of overgrown azalea hedges. But how many of their heated words (their own words, their private anger) do you need to prove your point? How will you answer their red-faced questions when they read your book?

That teacher is ruining your child's fourth-grade year. She has given him a D in Science not because of what he knows (damn it, he knows it all!) but because of his handwriting. She has thrown his books to the floor in despair over his still developing organizational skills. She has been called to task for her behavior by the principal himself. This may be essential to your story. This may be true. She may be all wrong, in fact, when it comes to your son. Do her the favor of keeping her name out of your book, for perhaps she's already pledged to do better next time. Perhaps she's already trying.

Your first boyfriend duped you. You'll never forgive him. You lost confidence and gained thirty pounds. Everything bad that happened after that—everything you were denied, everything you lost—goes straight back to the yellow-teethed, pockmarked, bad-dressing, you-can't-believe-you-ever-loved-him asshole. That is your story. You plan to tell it. You have a World-Class Epiphany all set for the end. But. Weigh the evidence again. Think tug-and-release. Tug. Release. There may well be more to this story and if you search empathetically for that bigger *more*, then your past—and that lousy, good-for-nothing, maybe-it-wasn't-in-fact-all-him dupe—may reveal itself newly. Your past may be more interesting. His character may be more complex. You'll have a better book.

I can't say it enough. To my students I never stop saying

it: You can't know what is going to offend, or mark, another. You can't foresee the many ways a book—even a small book, even a self-published one distributed to a mere dozen friends—will carry forward through your life and through the lives of others—leaving indentations here, scars there, a trail of tears, an infiltrated reputation. I speak from experience—five memoirs. I speak as one who has systematically sought permission for every line in a book that relates to another, and who has failed nonetheless. Reviewers will say what they will about your book. Readers will draw their own conclusions. You can think you've locked it all up tight, but unforeseen winds will blow through. The only thing you can control when writing memoir is what you actually say and how you prepare the ones you love for the book's journey into the world.

Empathy, then. For their sake. For yours. And finally for the sake of your art.

SEEK BEAUTY

I was the kid with the willow tree bark at her back and the blank-page book on her lap, writing sonnets to Zeus and his cohorts. I was cloud swept and purple saturated, tipped toward melody and song. I skated on ponds, and speed was a poem. I looked for meaning in the places where the hues of separate watercolors met and blurred. I sat on the bridge, watching the poor creek go by, desperate for something to say. Poetry was my ideal, a vast seduction. The way an image could be made to turn in on itself. The way sound itself was meaning. The economics of signifiers. The metering of intent. Complexity. Grace. Mystery. Intrigue. The fantastic smithereening and reconstituting of vocabulary itself. The inherent possibility that something original could be said. It was breathtaking. I wanted poetry for myself.

Just as I want memoir. Just as all that lives in a poem is possible—I believe this—with memoir. The endearing and the enduring. The subversive and the supposed. The ephemeral and the everlasting. The yelp and the yowl. The you within the me. This is what I love about memoir. This—like my son's face, like the ocean at dawn, like yellow wings in a blooming tree, like the cadence of a jungle hill, like a fleet of winter stars—is beauty to me.

Teach me how to write like this. It was my student Gabe who said it. He'd come to class early, carrying words a friend had written, and he'd asked me how sentences like those got made. Gabe was studying engineering. He knew process and mechanics. But here he was in my still-dark classroom, asking me to teach him beauty.

And so we moved through the opening lines of his friend's work, trying to discern where beauty lived. Where was momentum, and where was pause? Where were the oblique corners, the unexpected encounters, the phrases where the writing suggested mastery not just over topic but over harmony, too? Gabe had to know where the beauty lay—for him—before he could begin making beauty for himself. It's no different for you or for me.

Poetic beauty, Natalia Ginzburg wrote in the essay "My Craft," "is a composite of ruthlessness, arrogance, irony, carnal love, imagination and memory, of light and dark, and if we cannot achieve all of these together, our result will be impoverished, precarious, and scarcely alive." Do you agree?

Or does Larry Woiwode come closer to describing your ambitions for assimilating, fathoming, and writing life when he explains, in *A Step from Death*:

> My interweaving is on purpose, with the hope of holding you in one of its stopped-moments for a momentary glimpse of your own infinity. All experience is simultaneous, stilled and sealed in itself, and we manage daily by imagining we move from minute to minute, somehow always ahead. Our multiple selves collide at every second of

intersection, one or the other vying for supremacy,
the scars of the past flooding through the present
texture of our personality, and maturity is knowing how to govern the best combination of them.

Or is beauty, for you, bound up in rivering rhythms, in
cacophonic detail, in that one wise found word, in the use of
punctuation? Is your beauty simple? Is your beauty complex?
Does plainspokenness factor in, or a certain erudition?

At some point in nearly all of my classes, I will stop the
conversation and read out loud to my students. "Memoirists on food," I'll say, and then read from Gabrielle Hamilton, Chang-rae Lee, Bich Minh Nguyen, M. F. K Fisher,
and whomever else I might have in my fat stack. "Memoirists on childhood"—I'll make the pronouncement then read
the words of Annie Dillard, Orhan Pamuk, Elias Canetti.
On other days, "Memoirists on dying." On still others,
"Memoirists on fear." In between, "Memoirists on regret"
and "Memoirists on knowing" and "Memoirists on packing
for a trip" and "Memoirists who like lists" and "Jane Satterfield, memoirist, on mothers and daughters and distance."
Student by student, I will ask for choices. Which passages
appealed? Which sentences resonated? Was any of this, to
your ear, beautiful?

On other days, I will pull out my battered copy of Lia
Purpura's essay "Autopsy Report" and cycle it, passage by
passage, around the room, for the students to read to each
other.

I shall begin with the chests of drowned men,
bound with ropes and diesel-slicked. Their ears
sludge-filled. Their legs mud-smeared. Asleep below

deck when a freighter hit and the river rose inside
their tug. Their lashes white with river silt.

Do these words fit easily into your mouth? I ask. Can
you imagine writing like this? What would you look for,
where would your words go, were you to find yourself
(alive) in a morgue?

Somber days, winter weather days, I have silenced the
room and spun a disc—poets reading their own work, poets intoning. What resonates? I've asked simply. And then,
complexly, Why? Asking the students, as Robert Pinsky
says, "to hear language in a more conscious way."

Sometimes I invite the students to read their own work
aloud. Sometimes I invite them to allow others to read
their work for them. Do the words sound like they were
meant to sound? Are the words conforming to the author's
philosophy of beauty?

We cannot impose our ideas of beauty on another,
though we will inevitably try. We cannot insist that others
love what we do, though we can tantalize and seduce. We
can only ask that beauty be considered, measured, weighed,
pursued by all those writing life stories. We're talking about
memoir—an art form, not a treatise. We're primed for the
inhering and daring, for a story to feel new. We want to be
placed in possession of the bold sprout of a cracked seed.
We want to be trusted with it.

I leave you with Pablo Neruda. Perhaps you'll start
your search for beauty here:

It is very appropriate, at certain times of day or
night, to look deeply into objects at rest: wheels

which have traversed vast dusty spaces, bearing great cargoes of vegetables or minerals, sacks from the coal yards, barrels, baskets, the handles and grips of the carpenter's tools. They exude the touch of man and the earth as a lesson to the tormented poet. Worn surfaces, the mark hands have left on things, the aura, sometimes tragic and always wistful, of these objects, lend to reality a fascination not to be taken lightly.

. . . That is the kind of poetry we should be after, poetry worn away as if by acid by the labor of hands, impregnated with sweat and smoke, smelling of lilies and of urine, splashed by the variety of what we do, legally or illegally.

A poetry as impure as old clothes, as a body, with its food stains and its shame; with wrinkles, observations, dreams, wakefulness, prophecies, declarations of love and hate, stupidities, shocks, idylls, political beliefs, negations, doubts, affirmations, taxes.

MOST UNLONELY

I walk the campus every day before class—always a new direction, always some memory that I am stalking. One day I went the length of Locust Walk and out toward West Philadelphia, where a mod-looking bowling alley had been slipped inside a residential street and the dental school where I once worked had gained the face of new authority. One day, behind the medical school, I found a garden and a bridged-over pond and sat on its edge, recalling my freshman-year despair over failed titration labs, the defeating hugeness of biology lecture halls. I've haunted the Quad, where I once lived. I've studied the facades of fraternity houses. I've stood on the corner of Forty-second and Spruce, besieged by memories of the friend with whom I'd shared a passion for Russian history. I remember the room where he kept the books he sometimes stole. I remember the soup that he made from his mother's recipe. I remember his fascination with Tolstoy. I remember my betrayal. His. I walk, before I teach memoir, through the places I remember.

There was an afternoon, during my first year, when the air was dark and the sky was rain, and melancholy was my mood, Brillo my temper; I couldn't shake it. This was before I had taken up residency in that Victorian manse. This was the semester that I taught on the second floor of the cozy and intricately staired Kelly Writers House. I was remembering my mother, who had passed away not long before. I was imagining my son negotiating a university campus all his own. I was missing the book project that I'd set aside so that I might come to Penn and teach. My shoes were soaked through, and my umbrella was ineffectual, and the bag I carried across my shoulder was an ache upon my bones. I opened the door to find Jonathan waiting—a magazine on his lap and his long legs folded at liberal angles, like some Erector Set construction. He was, I thought, taking refuge from the storm. He rose when he saw me, began to climb the stairs beside me, and soon we were joined by another. When we reached the narrow hall just outside our classroom, we found Kim, who had arrived with a days-old kitten tucked into the collar beneath her chin. "They call him Wild Bill," she told us, "and I think he likes my bling," for this refugee from the streets of West Philly had dug his claws in deep to her necklace chain and was, it seemed, intent on staying, as most anyone who meets Kim is.

"We should just talk," Kim said, once we'd moved into our room. "At least to begin with." And because the room was dark and the skies were saturated, because Wild Bill had been whisked to some mysterious zone of safety, because the other students had, by now, come, we talked. About a recent campus suicide. About false diagnoses. About the places where the imagination lives. About reaching beyond the person one already is. We were each in our place, and we were holding on, for this is teaching, too—unquantifiable, and essential. And life is where memoir begins.

We turned, finally, to Terrence Des Pres, to his essays "Writing into the World" and "Accident and Its Scene: Reflections on the Death of John Gardner." Like so many before me, I am helplessly drawn to this man. His slender, groundbreaking exploration of community and generosity in Nazi death camps, *The Survivor*. The lovely lyric of his essays. His insistence that writers bear witness. Out loud I read Des Pres's reflections on John Gardner's ultimately inexplicable early death with a heart made heavy with the knowledge of Des Pres's own far-too-soon, and essentially unreadable, passing. I read about the faith Des Pres held in this strange and beautiful thing we writers do: "Few of us believe anymore that through art our sins shall be forgiven us, but perhaps it's not too much to think that through art a state of provisional grace can be gained, a kind of redemption renewed daily in the practice of one's craft." I read from "Ourselves or Nothing," the poem Carolyn Forché wrote to honor Des Pres, and these were our subjects this day. Provisional grace. Redemption renewed. The endless practice of our craft.

How does one speak of grief? I asked my students. To whom does such sadness belong? And is *knowing* what matters most of all, or does *wanting* to know matter more?

"Wanting," Kim said softly.

"Wanting," I agreed. "*Wanting* to know matters more."

Those who teach do not create, we're told. Those who give back will not be remembered for their genius. Those who love too much get nowhere. Those who cede the stage are thrust aside. That day the rain kept falling and the skies grew darker and we kept talking, my students and me. About life and books and secrets and questions, Terrence Des Pres and John Gardner, Carolyn Forché and Nazi camps, and memoir. Long after the quitting hour we said good-bye, and it was darker and even wetter by the time the train rattled me home. By ten o'clock that night, I was back at my desk when an e-mail from Jonathan came in. A note and an attachment.

> This is a brief article about my uncle that my mother forwarded to me this morning, and it seemed like a bizarre memoir of sorts—it's definitely not biographical, but more like a semi-connected series of anecdotes—all poorly translated into English. And even if it were translated properly, the tone is so distinctly foreign. At any rate, treated as a sort of memoir, I thought you might find it interesting. It seems almost like a very narrow window into a life that the author clearly has no understanding of, but is almost unconscious of that ignorance.

It was late, and I was tired. I opened the attachment and read. I was confused at first, thrust in, as had been promised, to a very foreign world. It wasn't until I reached the essay's end that I found this:

> During the duration of his teaching, he was noted as the most unlonely teacher. In the eyes of students, he did not look exactly like a teacher, when we mixed around with him, all of us would completely

forget his teacher position, and we really had established a true, honest and deep relationship.

"Most unlonely teacher." I read the words again. *Most unlonely.* For that is the privilege of teaching memoir, the privilege of reading memoir, the privilege of sometimes writing it—the community that rushes in as we tell stories that are true. "Aren't you tired of memoir yet?" I'll be asked, from time to time. "Don't you want to teach something else? Move on?"

"No," I'll say. "I'm not tired yet." Because I'm not done, and won't ever be. Because memoir will never be fully conquered. Because memoir is about life knowingly, thoughtfully lived. I will be the perpetual student and teacher of memoir until the last fleet of stars in the last night sky performs its light for me.

APPENDIX: READ. PLEASE.

YOU can teach yourself (or others) to see beyond what is near, to spend time with what you're not, to bear in mind the symphonic construction of a passage, to wait for an original idea. You can teach process: *Don't hurry.* You can teach living: *Go out, adventure, return.* You can fracture safety zones.

But the job of a teacher, most of all (I think), is to know what others have written and what another must read, right now, this second, in the midst of the long journey. The job of a teacher is to share.

Ever since I brought Natalie Kusz's *Road Song* home with me from a Princeton bookstore, I have had a bad memoir habit. Reading as many as I can, owning more than can fit on my shelves, dancing around untidy stacks. And complaining (my husband might say whining) that I have not read nearly what I want to read, nearly what *must* be read, of memoir.

It would therefore be preposterous for me to suggest that what I have assembled here is *the* categorical list of the best literary memoirs. I don't like the word *best* to begin with. It would be equally preposterous and unhelpful to suggest that memoirs can be locked into hard-and-fast categories. Obviously, *House of Prayer No. 2* is as much about childhood as it is about illness, but it is also about a man fleeing and then returning home. *Running in the Family* and *An American Childhood* are as much about how memories are assembled and how memoir gets made as they are about a certain place and time. Is *Father's Day* a celebration of a son or a book about grief? It is both things, of course. Is it fair to slip *Mentor* in with books about fathers, mothers, and children? I had to put it somewhere.

What follows, then, is a list of memoirs (and, only occasionally, memoiristic essay collections) from which I have learned, placed within categories that I hope will be generally useful. Memoirs that—whether I have agreed with their politics or utterly been won over by their perspective, whether they have gone too far or not far enough, whether I envy the life remembered or worry through it— *whether or not*—don't just offer insight into what it is to be human and to quest and to yearn, but also suggest stylistic, thematic, or structural possibilities to all those seeking to wade into the genre with their own inky pens uncapped. Something in each of these books will rankle, no doubt. Something or many things will be questioned—the number of adverbs, the resiliency of verbs, the excess of ego, the expanses of dialogue, the degree of masking, the inconsiderate consideration of private lives, the conclusions drawn. Perfection is not promised in my suggested reading list for this excruciating but as lovely reason: Perfection is not possible.

You will find your own memoirs to love. You will

wonder why some of your favorites are not on this list. You will complain to a friend. You will blog about my inevitable injustice.

But if you are doing that, you're reading.

That's what I want for you.

CHILDHOOD RELIVED

ROAD SONG/Natalie Kusz

The story of the author's long recovery from the ferocious attack of a pack of Alaskan dogs, *Road Song* is a revelation of form. Here is the past delivered with equanimity and respect. Here is a terrible tragedy gentled by words, a book in which the good is ever present with the bad. Natalie Kusz writes to comprehend, and not to condemn. She writes her way back to herself, and as she does, she broadens the reader's perspective, disassembles bitterness, heals. *Road Song* begins in the spirit of adventure, not with despair. *Road Song* begins with an *our* and not an *I* and reverberates out, like a hymn.

AN AMERICAN CHILDHOOD/Annie Dillard

In her classic memoir *An American Childhood*, Annie Dillard recounts the life she lived with an astonishing accretionary style. Starting with her tenth year, it seems, she remembers everything—the books she read "to delirium" and her youthful assessments ("*Native Son* was good, *Walden* was pretty good, *The Interpretation of Dreams* was okay, and *The Education of Henry Adams* was awful"); the rocks she collected and the lines they drew ("Yellow pyrite drew a black streak, black limonite drew a yellow streak"); even the faces of perfect strangers seen once but fleetingly ("A linen-suited woman in her fifties did meet my exultant eye"). Even as a child, Dillard felt the need to trap and remember—to record her life so that it wouldn't elude her, so that what she had lived would be eternally webbed to whom she would become. Readers of this memoir will be inspired to look back on their own lives and challenged to recollect and re-shimmer the signifying details.

THE LIARS' CLUB: A MEMOIR/Mary Karr

Mary Karr grows up living the hardest possible scrabble of a life, in a poisonous town, with a Nervous mother; with a daddy who excels at big, foggy stories among menfolk at the Liars' Club; with a grandmother whose dying from cancer is an unrelieved grotesquerie, and whose fake leg with its fake shoe terrifies a child who is herself ornery as anything, except when nobody's looking. Karr knows when to use the past tense and when to wing at us with the present. She understands that in a story this full of snakes and madness, accidents and fires, the crawl of sugar ants up the arm of a dying woman, she will only gain our trust by saying, sometimes, that maybe her memory has been fudged, or maybe her sister recalls it better, or maybe she'll just have to leave that part blank because her thoughts went blank at that particularly crucial moment. People write about *The Liars' Club*, and they write about its funniness, its love, which is all quite a trick, if you ask me. It's quite a trick to look back on what Mary Karr looks back on— poverty, abuse, danger, hurting of every measure—and come up with a story written not to tattle on what was done, not to complain, not to suggest that the author had it hard up—*See?*—but to try to understand what breed of sadness, heartache, or shatter might lie at the bottom of her mother's supreme but never evil oddness. Every sentence in this book is a poem, some daredevil twist on what we think language is. Essential.

AUTOBIOGRAPHY OF A FACE/Lucy Grealy

Lucy Grealy would not have wanted her memoir classified, and she especially would not have wanted it bucketed under "Unwell." And so I place this remarkable work here, for it is, in so many ways, a story about growing up and learning the scales and textures of a world, a story about seeing and transcending, a story about appearance and the accommodations one must make when disease—in this case a rare form of cancer discovered when Grealy was a child—reconfigures a face and restructures a life around dozens of surgeries and countless hospital stays. A large section of Lucy's jaw will be lost to the cancer. More than two years of her young life will be consumed by radiation and chemotherapy. Operations designed to restore symmetry to her face will fail, one way or the other, always. And Grealy will have to find a way—and she does find a way—to assert her beauty, her wisdom, her capacity for forgiveness, her writerly mind. Page after page of this masterful memoir has something to say, to all of us.

STOP-TIME: A MEMOIR/Frank Conroy

If one seeks proof of the power of scenes in memoir, one need look no further than *Stop-Time*, the story of Frank Conroy's rugged childhood and uncertain adolescence, first published in 1967. The careful orchestration of both past-tense and present-tense storytelling gives Conroy distance—and room—to walk around in his own life, to discover the themes, to find a way to understand, or to at least meet halfway, the father who stopped living with the family when Conroy was "three or four." It gives him a means, as well, to engage us. Prologue and epilogue are put to exceedingly good use in *Stop-Time*. Dialogue is proportionate, and credible.

SPEAK, MEMORY: AN AUTOBIOGRAPHY REVISITED/Vladimir Nabokov

". . . the individual mystery remains to tantalize the memoirist," Vladimir Nabokov writes in *Speak, Memory*. "Neither in environment nor in heredity can I find the exact instrument that fashioned me, the anonymous roller that pressed upon my life a certain intricate watermark whose unique design becomes visible when the lamp of art is made to shine through life's foolscap." No memoir is more richly sensed than Nabokov's, whose life story, episodically conveyed, confirms the power of images and patterns, symbols and color, unapologetic nostalgia and love.

AMERICAN CHICA: TWO WORLDS, ONE CHILDHOOD/Marie Arana

I love to read out loud from the start of *American Chica*—to inhabit its rich landscape of sounds, its sensual memory. Arana is an adult looking back on a childhood defined by a South American man and a North American woman—her parents. She is trying to make sense of their inevitable divide and where she fits between them. Every story Arana tells, every meditative pause, is written with the hope of understanding and with the recognition that we will never fully know all the secret yearnings of those who feathered our childhood homes. "They were so different from each other, so obverse in every way. I did not know that however resolutely they built their bridge, I would only wander its middle, never quite reaching either side."

THE GLASS CASTLE: A MEMOIR/Jeannette Walls

At the start of every semester, I ask my memoir students to bring a "best example" of memoir to class. Jeannette Walls's meditation on childhood survived inevitably makes an appearance. In terms of readerly popularity it is the memoir of our age, though I argue, with my students, that this fine work of writing might better be classified as autobiography, as is Frank McCourt's *Angela's Ashes*; the line in this case is quite thin. Walls's story is a character study of a father equally vibrant and annihilating, a free-spirited mother, and a daughter (Jeannette) who somehow doesn't just get by but moves forward, too, toward a life threaded through with a glamorous career, a lovely husband, and an attentive Park Avenue doorman. It's the full-bodied quality of *The Glass Castle* that escalated its popularity. Walls tells infinitely horrifying scenes without condemning the perpetrators. So that, for example, children idly experimenting with explosives or "nuclear fuel" and idly setting the walls around them on fire and finally running for their father will hear not yelling from their dad, not scolding threats, but rather a thoughtfully delivered lecture on "the boundary between turbulence and order."

FUN HOME: A FAMILY TRAGICOMIC/
Alison Bechdel

Alison Bechdel's graphic memoir about growing up Addams Family style in central Pennsylvania—her father not just a funeral home director and an English teacher but also a man secretly loving younger men; her mother sequestered in shame and small-town theater; her home gothic and wildly floral (thanks to her father)—is multitiered and searingly smart. This is a mixed-up family. The father comes to a terrible, uncertain end. Bechdel will never know if her own newly declared sexual orientation helped precipitate her father's death; she will never know a lot of things. That doesn't stop her from creating a warm, vulnerable, deeply knowing, utterly literate account of her own growing up. Webbed within seven superbly choreographed chapters, this is a gorgeous graphic memoir in which every word, myth, thought bubble, and citation counts.

BONE BLACK: MEMORIES OF GIRLHOOD/bell hooks

How did bell hooks (born Gloria Jean Watkins) become bell hooks—a poor black girl who finds her purpose as a poet and writer? How did books, old people, a priest, and a writer named Rilke save her? What does she see when she looks back; what are the refrains? What steeled her and softened her and almost thwarted her, but didn't? hooks calls this memoir a crazy quilt, and it is—intensely melodic, experimental, devoid of quotation marks, fluent in many versions of the grammatical pronoun, interested in the ways that the mind works, the patterns that return, the seams we sew for ourselves.

LIMBO: A MEMOIR/A. Manette Ansay

Limbo tells the story of A. Manette Ansay "learning to live" in the wake of a muscle disorder that suddenly (at the age of nineteen) renders every movement excruciating and a dream of becoming a concert pianist both implausible and painful. Ansay captures a childhood of great restlessness and yearning and transports her readers through the confusion of a religious upbringing that seeks to subdue the passions that Ansay knows to be true within herself. Time moves fluidly through this memoir. Wisdom is gained:

"Point of view is the vantage point from which the world is observed, the story is told. If that vantage point changes, the point of view *shifts*, and the story reshapes itself to accommodate the new perspective. One landscape is lost; another is gained. The distance between is called *vision*."

STEALING BUDDHA'S DINNER:
A MEMOIR/Bich Minh Nguyen

In the spring of 1975 South Vietnam was a place overrun with rumors of reeducation camps, torture, and extinction— a place where rockets shattered neighborhood calm and hulking tanks overtook cityscapes. Simply surviving meant taking risks—putting your children on American rescue helicopters, or finding your way onto a plane, or escaping in the dark hold of a ship. Some brave souls stayed and hid from the feared Communists. Many died in the terrifying chaos. In the midst of all of this was Bich Minh Nguyen's family—a father, his mother, his brothers, and two very little girls whose mother, having never married the father, lived across town. At the height of the terror, the Nguyens made a fateful, irreversible decision: to flee toward the unknown on a crowded boat that had been docked on the Saigon River. The author was eight months old when her family fled Saigon and barely a toddler upon her arrival in the States. She recalls, in *Stealing Buddha's Dinner*, the texture and the wonder of her new life in Grand Rapids and, in precise detail, the food. Nguyen understands the evocative possibilities of language, is fearless in asserting the specificities of memories culled from early childhood, and is herself an appealing character on the page.

MOTHERS, FATHERS, CHILDREN

RUNNING IN THE FAMILY/Michael Ondaatje

How can I convey to you just how exhilarated I am every time I sit down with Michael Ondaatje's *Running in the Family*—a pastiche of a memoir, a cobbling together of poems and artifacts, remembered conversations and new ones, antics and antiques, the incredible and the incredulous. This re-creation of a Sri Lankan childhood is steeped in exotica. It is lush and close-leaning. It is ripe with language. It provides yet another example of how much beauty can burst forth—sheer wonder—when we choose not to judge the people who raised us oddly but rather to marvel at their own idiosyncratic bearings and pain. If you want to know what memoir can be, read *Running in the Family*. If you want to see how memoir gets made, sit down and read it again. A favorite line: "My Grandmother died in the blue arms of a jacaranda tree. She could read thunder."

THE DUKE OF DECEPTION:
MEMORIES OF MY FATHER/Geoffrey Wolff

Few memoirs teach what memoir can be as gracefully as Geoffrey Wolff's *The Duke of Deception*. Leaving scolding and exhibitionism aside, evoking the past without summarizing it, *Duke* is a father-son story, a forgiveness story, an adventure, a lesson. Geoffrey Wolff's father hardly ever told the truth, and he was a wreck, and he wrecked things. He was a shameful disappointment, and he died ignoble, and yet every word in this breathtaking book is written from a place of love. Essential and forever timely.

ALL OVER BUT THE SHOUTIN'/Rick Bragg

You never forget Rick Bragg once you read his Southern tale. You won't forget his mother, either, and that's mostly Bragg's point, mostly his purpose in going back and reporting on the woman who raised this Pulitzer winner to be someone even as she denied herself every imaginable comfort. There is no end of fascination in this tale—the drunk, bullying, primarily absent father haunted by the Korean War; the mother who does her best; the grandparents and the townsfolk of the glorious and strange northeastern Alabama. There are glorious sentences here, big ideas about life and love that Bragg modestly calls small. *Shoutin'* is a love story for a deserving mother.

WHY BE HAPPY WHEN YOU COULD BE NORMAL?/Jeanette Winterson

Why Be Happy When You Could Be Normal? is the story, at first, of Mrs. Winterson, Jeanette's apocalyptic, domineering, supremely lonely and lonesome-making adoptive mother. Mrs. Winterson is a big woman among small people in an industrial town in northern England. She is a death dreamer and Bible reader, a fearless deliverer of obscenely unkind punishments, a practiced hypocrite. She figures large. She wields not just a metaphoric big stick but also an actual revolver. She sets traps and insists on irreversible consequences. Jeanette grows up with this. She finds her way to books. She's scrappy and wild and falls in love with girls. She makes her way, miraculously, until things fall apart and love proves elusive. Late in life—after great success as an artist, after breakdowns big and small—Jeanette sets out to find her birth mother. Jeanette would like to know what real love is, and if she herself is capable not just of giving it but of receiving it, too. Her journey won't be binary. Her discoveries will not be pat. Any attempt to summarize any of this goes straight up against the honest search of the book. Equally about becoming a woman and becoming a writer, this episodic memoir passes no judgment, finally. It merely (and essentially) absolves.

TOWNIE: A MEMOIR/Andre Dubus III

Townie is a long book, not one to be rushed through. It is a hard book, a tale about the fate of children growing up in the wake of an occasional dad—a talented man, a loving man, but a man who puts his impulses and his writing first. Andre Dubus II, the author's father, has, we come to realize (thanks to the son's telling), no real idea why his children are hungry or chased or being hurt in the world, or why his namesake son doesn't know how to throw a ball, or why that same son turns to beefing up and boxing and lashing out at the world that can do tremendous harm. Dubus III overcomes the embattled nature of his adolescent circumstance by clinging to his faith that the only defense he has (for himself, for his family) is muscle and fist. Throughout the book we see this kid (and, later, this man) throwing a sucker punch, knocking an enemy to the ground, riding in the back of a police car, sitting briefly behind bars, and hearing, later, that one of his victims was sent to the hospital, that one of the victim's friends is out to get him. Dubus has smashed through his own childhood. Urgently written, *Townie* is a reckoning. It is an insider's look at how one moves past fists toward words, past heartbreak toward compassion, and past broken family to a wholeness of one's own.

MISGIVINGS: MY MOTHER, MY FATHER, MYSELF/C. K. Williams

Misgivings offers an exploration of the spaces between the many unnamed things that happen in a life. There are no dates, no proper nouns, no specific locales divulged in *Misgivings*. There are no exhaustive reading lists, no revivals of perfect strangers, no cataloging of seasons or events, no maps drawn out of childhood homes, no allegiance to chronology. There isn't even a narrative arc. The dynamic here is that of memory and forgiveness, the way each acts upon the other to both restore and shatter. The plot is that of a man coming to terms with the parents that he had—the ways he loved them, the ways he did not, the ways he was shaped by who they were. An impeccable poet whose work has been awarded almost every conceivable honor, C. K. Williams does not back away from the life he's lived, does not hesitate to reveal the darker side of the legacy he inherited. And yet the brutal honesty of Williams's meditations does not negate the love he ultimately and so gorgeously finds for his parents, and between his parents, and among the three of them. Love is behind every word of this book. Love and Williams's final faith in it.

MENTOR: A MEMOIR/Tom Grimes

Tom Grimes's authoritative, unfancy, and bracingly honest memoir is about his relationship with Frank Conroy, who authored the classic and important memoir *Stop-Time* and headed the Iowa Writers' Workshop. Grimes came into Conroy's orbit as a student—as a man waiting tables and writing at night, a man desperate to make a literary life. Grimes becomes, quite quickly, someone more—someone Conroy can drink with, talk to, and selflessly encourage. And oh, does Conroy selflessly encourage. He urges Grimes on; he connects him to possibilities; he celebrates Grimes's good moments and is there to buffer the bad. Many writers—too many writers—focus only on themselves, their own work, their own fame. Conroy clearly was not that sort, and Grimes's portrait of him is illuminating and restorative.

THEN AGAIN/Diane Keaton

Celebrities tend to write autobiographies. Diane Keaton didn't. She wants to understand who her mother is, how her mother shaped her, and what kind of mother she herself is now, and to do this, Keaton artfully poses the right questions and, taking risks, leaves aside that which does not matter. She is quiet, unassuming, funny, graceful, and one believes she is telling the truth. She did not write to entertain us, per se. She takes no easy potshots. She gives us the men she loved for the reasons she loved them. She gives her yearning, sometimes depressed, slowly fading mother the room for her own story. Keaton writes because she is one of us. She writes to find her way. This is not a book of quips or anecdotes or gossip. It's life, and it's beautifully rendered—a book that takes great structural risks to astonishingly moving effect.

THE FLORIST'S DAUGHTER: A MEMOIR/
Patricia Hampl

"Middle-class, Midwestern, midcentury—middle everything"—that was Patricia Hampl's lot in life. Born to a Czech florist and his Irish wife, raised in St. Paul as the second child of two, Hampl grew up like so many of us did—looking for escape, circling right back around to home. She went fishing with her father. She whisked across slicked ice rinks. She listened to her mother's stories. She wanted out. She didn't go. "A son is a son until he takes a wife. A daughter is a daughter all her life"—that was her mother's mantra. That was Hampl's fate. It is also the subject of her memoir, *The Florist's Daughter,* which is neither a settling of accounts nor a deification. Hampl isn't searching for heroes in *The Florist's Daughter.* She's listening for echoes, affixing shadows, taking a tour of her memory again, the photos again, the stories she'd been told again, and also the lies that she was fed and that she harbored. Hampl isn't on a hunt for pity. She's testing the limits of understanding. *The Florist's Daughter* reminds us that we don't understand what it is to grow old until we are asked to take that journey with our parents. It yields perspective. It makes sitting, waiting, aching, and watching honorable, and restores our sense of purpose.

TWO OR THREE THINGS
I KNOW FOR SURE/Dorothy Allison

To hold this memoir in your hand is to hold something birdlike, fierce, and fragile. The words are widely spaced. Photographs float across the ecru pages. Declarations are cried out; they vanish. There are two or three things that Dorothy Allison knows for sure about her Southern childhood; her wounded, wounding people; her own bold instincts; her refusal to bend to shame, to be put down by it. Two or three things, far more than two or three things, and this book is an effort to write them down, to keep them in place, to sing out loud, to work past the abuse she suffered in childhood. "When I make love I take my whole life in my hands, the damage and the pride, the bad memories and the good, all that I am or might be, and I do indeed love myself, can indeed do any damn thing I please," Allison writes. "I know the place where courage and desire come together, where pride and joy push lust through the blood-stream, right to the heart." *Two or Three Things* is a chant, a rising, euphonic suite of epiphanies.

FATHER'S DAY: A JOURNEY INTO THE MIND AND HEART OF MY EXTRAORDINARY SON/Buzz Bissinger

Buzz Bissinger's book is a memoir about fatherhood and about a trip he took with his adult son Zach, a second-born twin who suffers from broad and not easily labeled differences. This is a book about not wanting and not getting, about bewilderment and exhilaration, about doing wrong and being wronged and loving hard and forever. It's raw and it's original, unafraid of the true impossible mess of life. On every page is proof of how an honest struggle, a desperate wrestling down, can at times yield a book that will be read for ages—not just for the story and for the wisdoms (which are many, accruing, and right), not just for the language (which is gorgeous as it both lances and limns), not just for the perfectly constructed asides that teach us the history of premature babies and savants, but also for the lessons it teaches about what can happen when we stop trying so hard to understand so that we might more simply live.

THE GIFT OF AN ORDINARY DAY: A MOTHER'S MEMOIR/Katrina Kenison

I'm simply going to share here what I wrote when I blurbed this book for my friend Katrina Kenison. I don't think anything more needs to be said: "With an honesty and intimacy rarely achieved in modern memoir, Katrina Kenison dissolves yearning into its complex, sensate parts. This is a book about midlife want and loss. It is also a most knowing book about a most gracious love—about the gifts that are returned to those who find beauty where it falls."

GRIEF

JUST KIDS/Patti Smith

Just Kids is advertised primarily as the story of rock legend Patti Smith's relationship with the artist Robert Mapple-thorpe, and that it is. But it is also the story of Smith's ascension through art—the years she spent choosing between buying a cheap meal or an old book, between being an artist or a writer, between being Mapplethorpe's lover or his best friend. She tells us about the conversations that generate ideas among artists and friends, about coincidences that set a life on its path, about the clothes she wore and the misimpressions she couldn't correct, about a kind of love that is bigger than any definition the world might want to latch onto it. She yields an entire era to us, and though her writing is all sinew, strength, and honesty, she does not once betray her friends, does not invite us to imagine privacies that should remain beyond the veil.

AN EXACT REPLICA OF A FIGMENT OF MY IMAGINATION: A MEMOIR/Elizabeth McCracken

A baby—planned for, deeply wanted, full term, dubbed (at least for that time being) Pudding—goes silent and still shortly before he is born. He will never see the sun; never know the parents who could not wait to begin their lives as a family of three; never see that part of France that had, until then, sustained his mother. Novelist Elizabeth McCracken will not write the story of Pudding's loss until Gus, her second son, is born. The coupling of these two stories—life denied and life given—is the substance and structure of *An Exact Replica of a Figment of My Imagination*. Grief—how we name it, how we tangle with it, how we look to others with need and unknowing, and how others turn back toward us, or do not—may saturate these pages, but it does not define them. Mc-Cracken goes deeper. With tremendous skill and honorable restraint, she evokes love. She tells us how it feels.

LET'S TAKE THE LONG WAY HOME: A MEMOIR OF FRIENDSHIP/Gail Caldwell

Gail Caldwell's finely crafted, thoroughly beautiful, absolutely heartbreaking *Let's Take the Long Way Home* is the story of Caldwell's rare friendship with the writer Caroline Knapp—the story of long walks taken with beloved dogs; of the glass face of rowed-upon water; of pasts and imperfections and desires entrusted, one to the other; of a cancer diagnosis and a death, Caroline Knapp's, when she was at the prime of her life and the center, in so many ways, of Caldwell's world. *Home* is a memoir filled with perfectly wrought particulars: "I often went out in early evening, when the wildlife had settled and the shoreline had gone from harsh brightness to Monet's gloaming, and then I would row back to the dock in golden light, the other scullers moving like fireflies across the water." *Home* is not a tale about how Caldwell survived the loss of her best friend, though Caldwell has survived. It is instead both instruction and allegory on the power of kindness and small gestures, the fidelity of friendship and memory, the tenacity and tenuousness that make us our own complicated people in need of other complicated people.

HEAVEN'S COAST: A MEMOIR/Mark Doty

In April 1993, Mark Doty looked toward a future of loss; Wally, his longtime lover, was dying of AIDS. Their life together was ending, or would soon end, and Doty tried to conceive of the future—make some peace with it—while living the days the couple had left. How do you celebrate and mourn at the same time? How do you hold on when you can't? Doty's memoir is a beautiful exercise in near balance— lyrical, philosophical, raw: "The future's an absence, a dark space up ahead like the socket of a pulled tooth. I can't quite stay away from it, hard as I may try. The space opened up in the future insists on being filled with *something*: attention, tears, imagination, longing."

HALF A LIFE: A MEMOIR/Darin Strauss

Half a Life is the story of an accidental death—the story of what happened one day when Strauss set out to play some "putt-putt" with his high school friends. He was eighteen, behind the wheel of his father's Oldsmobile. On the margin of the road, two cyclists pedaled forward. Of a sudden, there was a zag, a knock, a "hysterical windshield." A cyclist, a girl from Darin Strauss's school, lay dying on the road. She'd crossed two lanes of highway to reach Strauss's car. He braked, incapable of forestalling consequences. It was forever. It was always. A girl had died. A boy had lived. Strauss spent his college years, his twenties, his early thirties incapable of reconciling himself to the facts, of entrusting them to friends. There's much he can't remember perfectly. There are gaps, white space, breakage—all of which are rendered with utmost decency, the thoughts broken into small segments, big breaths (blank pages) taken in between.

THE LONG GOODBYE: A MEMOIR/ Meghan O'Rourke

One expects from poets deeply lyrical, language-invested memoirs, especially when the topic is grief—or at least I do. But in *The Long Goodbye*, this very personal but also deliberately universal story about losing her fifty-five-year-old mother to cancer, the poet Meghan O'Rourke chooses language that is almost stark, rarely buoyed by metaphor, and frequently amplified by the words of experts to retrace her journey through loss. O'Rourke wasn't prepared for her mother's absence. Can anyone be? She has lost something, and she continues to look—avidly, stonily, ragingly, insistently. She reads the literature. She talks with friends. She risks bad behavior simply to find the prickle of living again. But O'Rourke, like all of us, has to live her grief alone, and the worst thing about grief, in the end, is this: There is no cure.

BLUE NIGHTS/Joan Didion

I was harder on Joan Didion's *The Year of Magical Thinking* than many readers were. I thought it at times too self-consciously clinical, too reported, less felt. Many of my students at the University of Pennsylvania disagreed with me. I listened, wanting to be convinced. Thankfully, I do not feel disinclined toward *Blue Nights*. The jacket copy describes the book as "a work of stunning frankness about losing a daughter." It is that; in part it is. But it is also, mostly, as the jacket also promises, Didion's "thoughts, fears, and doubts regarding having children, illness, and growing old."

A cry, in other words, in the almost dark. A mind doing what a mind does in the aftermath of grief and in the face of the cruelly ticking clock. *Blue Nights* is language stripped to its most bare. It is the seeding and tilling of images grasped, lines said, recurring tropes—not always gently recurring tropes. It is a mind tracking time. It is questions. It isn't easy reading; it's hardly that. But it is stunning, sometimes stirring.

THE TENDER LAND: A FAMILY LOVE STORY/Kathleen Finneran

With *The Tender Land*, Kathleen Finneran is asking vast, impossible questions about love and loss. She is restoring a long-lost brother to the page, a boy named Sean, who killed himself at the age of fifteen for reasons no one can fathom. Why did Sean swallow his father's heart medicine? Who was responsible for his sadness? What should Finneran herself have known to protect this brother from his fate? These are personal questions, certainly, very particular details, one family, one love, one loss. But as Finneran tells her story, she urges her readers deep into themselves, asks them to consider those whom they, too, love, and whether or not they have loved fully enough. Finneran's fine prose operates as a prayer—for both her brother and her readers.

PAULA: A MEMOIR/Isabel Allende

"Listen, Paula. I am going to tell you a story, so that when you wake up you will not feel so lost." So begins Isabel Allende's deeply affecting love letter—memoir—to her daughter, Paula, a young woman who has fallen into a coma at a time when life should be dazzled with possibility. Of course Allende's tale wends crooked and possibly untrue. Of course there are fantastical things and phantasmagoria.

Of course the book is far more about Allende than it is about her daughter, but this is memoir, and this is what grief looks like to one of the most imaginative storytellers of our time. Paula speaks to Allende in dreams. Paula is slipping away. All the stories in the world can't save her, nor can Allende's confessions. What there is at the end is an act of love—a mother sitting near, bearing witness, to the hardest thing of all.

DEVOTION: A MEMOIR/Dani Shapiro

In the elegant prose of Dani Shapiro, *devotion* is another word for *quest*. It is the journey to know—and to reckon with not knowing—how one lives in a world of risks, in a body aging, in the vessel of uncertainty. Having reached the middle-middle of her life, having left the city for the country, having raised a little boy who beat the odds of a rare and dangerous disorder, having achieved much as both a novelist and a memoirist (and also a screenwriter), Dani Shapiro wakes from her sleep full of worries and lists. Her jaw quakes. Her thoughts slide. She gets caught up in the stuff of life and then—and then—she worries. Shapiro was the child of a deeply religious household, and she doesn't know what she believes. She is the mother of a boy asking questions, simple, impossible questions about God and heaven and sin. She should know something, shouldn't she? She should have something definitive to offer. But what, in the end, is rock-solid, sure? What bolsters us, protects us, from vicissitudes and chance? Sentence by sentence, this is a beautiful book—considered and pure. Structurally, it is magnificent, scenes abutting scenes, time cutting into time, small threads woven into a greater tapestry. We never really do have more than one another, and that is what Shapiro comes to. Shapiro's book, itself, is a hand outstretched, an open door, a place to dwell.

BEREFT: A SISTER'S STORY/Jane Bernstein

Jane Bernstein, "a child who stood in doorways, heart beating hard," was always watchful, always a listener—and perhaps too obedient. When her older sister was murdered by a stranger, Jane, then seventeen, does what her mother advised by getting "right back into the swing of things." More than two decades pass before Jane's daughter asks a question about her aunt Laura—and sends Jane into a journey of discovery. What did happen to her sister? How had Laura's death shaped Jane's own life? What could be known, and what would never be? Part detective story, part reckoning, this complex memoir weaves across decades and through themes without ever losing its center.

THE NATURAL WORLD

Memoirs are about people first, but people arise from, move through, and finally return to landscapes. Many of the best writers about the natural world are personal essayists, masters of the short form. We come to know their stories episodically; we don't necessarily look for continuums. In constructing this list I chose to include a few titles that would more properly be shelved among essay collections. This is because these books contain passages and insights that are relevant to any memoirist working the long form.

PILGRIM AT TINKER CREEK/Annie Dillard

"I walk out; I see something, some event that would otherwise have been utterly missed and lost; or something sees me, some enormous power brushes me with its clean wing, and I resound like a beaten bell." That's the inimitable Annie Dillard writing. That's a single quotable passage out of countless quotable passages in her Pulitzer Prize–winning *Pilgrim at Tinker Creek*. This is a book about seeing, harboring, honoring—a book about being aware. What happens when we stop and look? Why are we all so afraid of letting "our eyes be blasted forever"?

REFUGE: AN UNNATURAL HISTORY OF FAMILY AND PLACE/Terry Tempest Williams

I found Terry Tempest Williams's *Refuge* in the days just after 9/11, when I was looking for a way to mourn all those lost and for those who lost them. The skies above were blue and silent. The birds in nearby trees were stubborn, without song. I stared up into a lanky birch; it was a tower. I saw the bloom of a new cloud; it was a plume of smoke. How do we mourn? There are answers in *Refuge*, a book about how Williams comes to terms with her own mother's dying and with the cruel incursions of pollution in the natural landscape she loves. "Particles of sand skitter across my skin, fill my ears and nose," she writes. "I am aware only of breathing. The workings of my lungs are amplified. The wind picks up. I hold my breath. It massages me. A raven lands inches away. I exhale. The raven flies." In *Refuge*—infinitely worth reading for both its language and its intelligence—Williams reminds us that "peace is the perspective found in patterns. . . . My fears surface in my isolation. My serenity surfaces in my solitude."

THE NAMES OF THINGS: LIFE, LANGUAGE, AND BEGINNINGS IN THE EGYPTIAN DESERT/Susan Brind Morrow

Susan Brind Morrow's *The Names of Things* is an exquisite example of the memoir form—a book of escape and discovery, exhaustion and surrender and relief. Morrow's book takes readers out far beyond where most have ever been—to the sands of Egypt, to the company of exotic beasts and plants—and somehow yields up passages that speak directly to the experience of humankind. "I thought of memory as a blanket," Morrow writes of her traveling days. "I could take a thing out of my mind and handle it as though it were part of some beautiful fabric I carried with me, things that had happened long ago, the faces of people I loved, the words of a poem I had long since forgotten I knew. This was something any nomad or illiterate peasant knew: the intangible treasure of memory, or memorized words." Morrow's readers don't have to go to Egypt to make this discovery. Morrow has made it for them, and has loved it with words, for their sake.

THE GOOD GOOD PIG: THE EXTRAORDINARY LIFE OF CHRISTOPHER HOGWOOD/
Sy Montgomery and Genine Lentine

Sy Montgomery's adventures to exotic corners of the world have brought us news of pink dolphins and golden moon bears. With her memoir, Montgomery stayed close to home to tell us the story of her 750-pound pet pig named Christopher, whose heart is bigger than his belly. Endearing and effusive, this memoir is full of love for those furry or squawking or barking or snorting creatures with which we share the world. It's full of observations, too, about how to live among four-legged souls. "Christopher Hogwood came home on my lap in a shoe box," the memoir begins. And as Christopher grows, so does our affection for him.

THE WILD BRAID: A POET REFLECTS ON A CENTURY IN THE GARDEN/Stanley Kunitz and Genine Lentine

Stanley Kunitz was one of the nation's most beloved and honored poets, and he lived for a very long time. Written toward the very end of his life, *The Wild Braid* is not just graceful and soulful; it is authentic, too, and with memoir, as we have observed, that matters. The book revolves around a house Kunitz bought back in 1962—a summer home the poet shared with his wife, Elise, until her passing. It revolves, more particularly, around the garden that, Kunitz tells us, was built from almost nothing, a "starkly barren area with nothing growing on it, not even grass." Building the garden entailed the digging in of seaweed and peat moss and manure, the construction of terraces, the planting and tending of flowers, and the constant management of the tension that pulses between faith and watchfulness. Garden and poetry— the two things are braided here, building, inexorably, to a greater understanding about life, a prayer.

A PRIVATE HISTORY OF AWE/
Scott Russell Sanders

As he sorts through the first six decades of his life, Scott Russell Sanders trains his focus on those moments when something telling happened, something that advanced his understanding of the world and of that condition— "rapturous, fearful, bewildering"—known as awe. Sanders wants his readers alert to the power of thunderstorms and baby sighs, to "the holy shimmer at the heart of things." He remembers himself as a boy on a Tennessee farm, his needing to know the names and tastes and shapes of whatever was near. Those memories live within the reality of present time—an aged and confused mother, an intensely curious child, a still insatiable desire to know.

WILD COMFORT: THE SOLACE OF NATURE/Kathleen Dean Moore

"This is a book about the comfort and reassurance of wet, wild places," Kathleen Dean Moore tells us in the introduction to *Wild Comfort*. Moore had, she reveals, set out to write a book about happiness, but then people she loved died, and the world took on a different hue, and nature—its colors, breezes, infinite surprises—became an even more steady and significant companion. This is, properly speaking, a collection of memoiristic essays. It is also a way to understand the natural world and our place in it to begin. An example: "I doze on wet grass and imagine myself part of the mysterious unfolding of the universe, imagine that inflorescence. I fit in here. Literally. I am one unfolding among other interfoldings and enfoldings, the wrinkled lap and pucker of life in Earth, the vulture and the possum and the dew on the plums."

THE RURAL LIFE/Verlyn Klinkenborg

There's an old-fashioned elegance to the shape of Verlyn Klinkenborg's sentences, a steady, transcendent, unshowy intelligence that one instinctively leans toward and trusts. Klinkenborg chronicles life as he knows it: a small-town parade, a change in the weather, a conversation with two old brothers down the road. The anecdotal claims his attention, the nearly incidental. Baling twine and barn swallows. Mosquitoes and a pumpkin patch. The way people plan for winter or, conversely, plan for spring.

The Rural Life is a compilation of the columns and essays he has published on such topics over the past several years. It's the last lines of these essays that readers should pay special attention to—lines I find to be arresting, even profound; lines that force us to look at the world in a new way.

UNWELL

THE MUSIC ROOM: A MEMOIR/
William Fiennes

Memoir writers and teachers should know about the castle in which William Fiennes grew up, and how it shaped him. They should know about his brother Richard, who suffered from severe epilepsy, lived for Leeds United soccer games, exalted the flight of herons, and erupted with anger before he retreated—confused, ashamed? There were other siblings and other tragedies in this ancient place. There were also two parents who honored Richard for what he could be and gave him everything he was capable of receiving. There is a hush throughout this book—a tumble through past and present, a drift across *here we were* and *here we are*, time in a collision with time. There are long slides of description regarding a castle that cannot be contained by words, or mapped, and then, embedded, are scenes of aching, particular precision—Richard tracks a heron, Richard skates on a frozen moat, Richard burns his mother with a frying pan, Richard sings, Richard smashes ancient glass,

Richard accuses, Richard lays a heavy (loving) hand upon Mum, Richard will not bathe, Richard celebrates Leeds, Richard recites a poem from memory, Richard suffers, William is there, William watches, William wonders. Then, like marks of punctuation (something solid, something fixed), there are episodic histories of epilepsy science, the scarred and fuming brain revealed.

THE DIVING BELL AND THE BUTTERFLY:
A MEMOIR OF LIFE IN DEATH/
Jean-Dominique Bauby

A mere 132 large-type pages long, *The Diving Bell and the Butterfly* is sensuous and steeped. Jean-Dominique Bauby, the former *Elle* editor, rendered locked-in by a massive stroke and speaking through the blinking of one eye. Letters read off to him until he consents to one and then another. Words congealing. Story. Hope. Most of us are blessed with hands that grip pens, fingers that do our bidding on keyboards. And yet we are, perhaps, tempted to hurry through scenes for the love of writing the next one, or to subsume a detail not readily recalled, or to rely on a familiar turn of phrase because the melody is familiar. Bauby's book serves as a reminder of what a man blinking each letter into place can achieve with language and with heart. His book teaches, at the same time, the riveting effects of wisely manipulated past and present tense. A book about irreparable loss and the buoyancy of remembering.

THE NIGHT OF THE GUN: A Reporter
Investigates the Darkest Story of His Life. His Own.
David Carr

By his own admission, David Carr was a substance abuser of the very first order—a "maniac" who went from handling whiskey and cocaine (barely) to not handling crack to smacking women he loved with an open hand to raising twins while failing at rehab to carrying a gun he doesn't remember, or didn't remember until he started tracking down his own past. Like the scrupulous *New York Times* reporter he miraculously became, Carr sought out and interviewed those whose lives intersected his during his wilderness years. He weighed his idea of things against police records and the recall of old friends. He sorted, sifted, and spun in an attempt to understand not just who he was, but who he is, and how the was and the is somehow survive inside the same knocked-about skin. It's fascinating reading, memoir painstakingly stitched. It has a lot to say about what truth is and what to do with all the stuff we can't rightly remember.

THE MEMORY PALACE: A MEMOIR/Mira Bartók

This is a daughter's story (for Mira Bartók is mostly, in her memoir, a daughter) about a brilliant, beautiful, mentally ill mother. It is a survival story, first and foremost—a deeply loving, never condemning return to a life spent looking for safety during a mother's unruly outbursts. This mother and her two daughters are poor to begin with; Mira's father abandons the family early on. But true poverty sinks in as their mother quickly loses her power to work and her ability to provide. The quiet days are the days when their mother is institutionalized. The terrifying days are the ones in which the mother leaves the girls stranded in places both foreign and familiar, or bangs on the other side of a door, demanding to know if the girls are whores. There is a grandmother nearby, but she has troubles of her own. There are neighbors and the occasional piano teacher or kind adult who step in, offering only temporary reprieves. Bartók, who is also a children's author, fills her story with allusions to myths and fantasy, softening the insufferable with flights of tremendously fancy. She writes at times quite simply and at times with a poet's stance. She blames no one, but always tries to understand. I admire her work enormously here—her empathy, her powers of recall—and if at times I felt that some of the tangents unnecessarily complicate the story, or take the tale as a whole more toward autobiography than memoir, I closed the book with respect for Bartók, not just as a writer but as a person, too.

DARKNESS VISIBLE: A MEMOIR OF MADNESS/William Styron

"In Paris on a chilly evening late in October of 1985 I first became fully aware that the struggle with the disorder in my mind—a struggle which had engaged me for several months—might have a fatal outcome." So begins William Styron's taut, harrowing exploration of a condition that will haunt him for years: depression. He doesn't favor the term. He fights against its stereotypes. But he also systematically works to understand what this disorder is doing to him, what it has done to others, and how the wrong "cures" can deepen despair.

AN UNQUIET MIND: A MEMOIR OF MOODS AND MADNESS/Kay Redfield Jamison

When Kay Redfield Jamison, a renowned expert on manic-depressive illness, released her memoir in 1995, she wasn't just helping others understand what this devastating disorder is and does; she was telling us what it's like to live through it—to survive. She had struggled with the condition herself as a teen.

She grew up veering left to right, somber to blazing, nearly out of control, and so smart. It's a very personal book—a searing story. It is also an enormously helpful book for those trying to understand and support others whose brain chemistries rocket them off toward trembling heights and melancholic lows.

GIRL, INTERRUPTED/Susanna Kaysen

It would have been simple (perhaps) for Susanna Kaysen to reconstruct her nearly two years at McLean Hospital among young women diagnosed as sociopaths and schizophrenics, former addicts and depressives. It would have, for many, been enough. But Kaysen never set out to write autobiography—to merely summarize an untamed time, to offer an explanation for her trauma. She set out to make art—to produce a memoir of many effective parts. Case file reports. Artful impressions of fellow patients. Sobering personal assessments. Definitions lifted from a diagnostic manual. White space. Smart chapter titles. Overt challenges of societal prejudices. An extraordinary absence of self-pity. "People ask, How did you get in there?" Kaysen begins. "What they really want to know is if they are likely to end up in there as well. I can't answer the real question. All I can tell them is, It's easy."

THE RULES OF THE TUNNEL: MY BRIEF
PERIOD OF MADNESS/Ned Zeman

A second-person tour de force, Ned Zeman's rumination on years scrambled by anxiety, depression, and mania; therapy, medication, and a trip to McLean; and, ultimately, treatment-triggered amnesia is a remarkable work of literature—raucous, ribald, fused together with profound insight and rare humor. It is also, as memoir must be, a conversation with the reader. This is what happened, writes

Zeman, an award-winning journalist and contributing writer at *Vanity Fair*. And this is how.

INTOXICATED BY MY ILLNESS/Anatole Broyard

Anatole Broyard is dying, and he is, at first, oddly intoxicated by the notion. "Suddenly there was in the air a rich sense of crisis—real crisis, yet one that also contained echoes of ideas like the crisis of language, the crisis of literature, or of personality," he tells us up front. "It seemed to me that my existence, whatever I thought, felt, or did, had taken on a kind of meter, as in poetry or in taxis." He seeks a "literature of illness." He uses his writing to counteract his illness—or likes to believe that writing has that power. But as this narrative evolves, it is clear that Broyard will not win against his disease. What Broyard does win, however, is the sense that he has lived until the very end. Broyard's truthfulness as a man, his willingness to live honestly within his own skin, was, of course, questioned after his death. This memoir remains elucidating for all the reasons mentioned here.

LEAVING AND RETURNING

HOUSE OF PRAYER NO. 2: A WRITER'S JOURNEY HOME/Mark Richard

You grow saddened, out here in life, by all the humdrum and the done before, the standard issue, the colors shimmed off to gray. So when you pick up a book like *House of Prayer No. 2*, a Mark Richard memoir rendered in meaty second-person prose, you let a smile crawl across your face and stay. Of course, you have to have a life like his to tell a true story like this: poor and "special," hips whacked out, days lost to the hopeless heat of a hospital for crippled children, and, afterward, everything you hope your child doesn't do, doesn't get involved with, doesn't risk—all that done, by Richard, on his way to growing up, on his way to faith and writing.

BROTHER, I'M DYING/Edwidge Danticat

Memoirs that make room for family history and national politics challenge their writers structurally; they ask more from the words on the page. No false binding will do, no obvious superimpositions, no easy themes, no ready truths. There are higher stakes in memoirs like these. More is expected, more wanted. In *Brother, I'm Dying*, Edwidge Danticat forges a remarkable narrative, establishing herself as her memoir's maker and not its heroine—there is such an important difference.

Intelligent, researched, heartfelt, the book weaves together the story of the man who raised Danticat as a child in Bel Air, Haiti—her uncle—and the man who fled to Brooklyn in an effort to create for his whole family a better life—her father. Two brothers, then, two father figures, and two ultimately tragic trajectories as each man fights to survive impossible odds and this daughter fights hard not to lose them. In a single year, 2004, Danticat—now married, in Miami, pregnant with her daughter—will watch her world unravel. She will bear witness to what revolutionary upheaval and disease can do to the men who, for so much of her youth, were not just essential but also invincible. She will find a way to make of fragments a whole.

A THREE DOG LIFE: A MEMOIR/Abigail Thomas

There is a very good reason that Stephen King called this memoir the best he'd ever read. It manages, at the very same time, to be spare and to offer great depth, to be intimate and somehow not self-involved, to be harrowing and also humorous (and also uplifting), to be about loss and yet (always) about the glorious possibilities of life right now, with whatever we still have, as whomever we still are. Abigail Thomas's husband went out one night to walk their dog. He didn't return. He had been struck by a car and badly hurt. His brain would never be the same. For the next many years he would live at a residential center and come home one day each week, and what could Abigail do but go about living in the meantime, hunting down beauty in her world, taking care of her three dogs, listening for the odd pearls of dreams or premonitions that the man she loved would sometimes share? This isn't continuous narrative so much as interlude. This is a book about living gracefully. A book about loving true.

MY INVENTED COUNTRY:
A MEMOIR/Isabel Allende

"I wrote my first book by letting my fingers run over the typewriter keys," Isabel Allende tells us toward the end of this memoir, "just as I am writing this, without a plan." So yes, this memoir rambles, and yes, its premise is suspect (the author vaguely suggests but never convincingly explores some sort of existential link between her exile from Chile and the tragedy at the World Trade Center), and yes, it treads familiar ground (Allende's famously eccentric and colorful family; Allende's notoriously stubborn and passionate personal life; Allende's fixation on Chile, where so much of her nostalgia is centered; Allende's views on the role of stories in our lives). But don't let any of that dissuade you from reading these earthy and seductive pages. Fabulously well endowed with detail and insight, *My Invented*

Country is willing to reckon with the ghosts and spirits that have inspired her oeuvre. "My tendency to transform reality, to invent memory, disturbs me," she writes, "I have no idea how far it may lead me. . . . Thanks to it, I found a voice and a way to overcome oblivion, which is the curse of vagabonds like me."

DRINKING: A LOVE STORY/Caroline Knapp

There isn't the bravado, in *Drinking*, of the Magnificent Survivor. There isn't the boast one sometimes hears in the recounting of harrowing tales—*Can you believe I was like that? Can you imagine I survived? I know it's nasty, I know I was a jerk, but secretly, really, wasn't it all kind of wondrous, in a twisted (I'll admit it) way?* There isn't the sense that Caroline Knapp believes that her story—about living with drink, about being tormented by it, about recognizing the need for sobriety and being terrified of coming to terms with her sober self—trumps all other tales. There is only the sense that perhaps by telling her tale—by exploring the slide, the massive deceptions, the dangers, the heat and seeming loveliness of alcohol—she may be helpful to others. This is not memoir as exorcism or exhibitionism, in other words. It's not a memoir in which the rememberer pretends to remember any more than she actually does. It is a book that is moving and hopeful and sad. It is authentic, as memoir must be.

THE MAP OF MY DEAD PILOTS:
THE DANGEROUS GAME OF FLYING
IN ALASKA/Colleen Mondor

This is the story of the four years Colleen Mondor spent running operations for a bush commuter airline in Fairbanks, Alaska. It's about the planes that rose and fell, the pilots that went missing, the cargo no one would believe. It's about defying the odds, the weather, the smash wall of mountains until those things rise up and speak and refuse to be defied. It's about vanishing, about vanishing's speed. It's about a daughter who loses her father too soon and who, in the end, writes stories down in search of some salvation. It's a memoir, but it's a chorus. It's a we and a them on the rhythmic order of Tim O'Brien's *The Things They Carried*, a book that brings us into itself (and keeps us there, utterly absorbed). This is that other kind of memoir in which the author is not the heroine but the webber, the weaver, the voice for those who are no longer here to tell their own stories. That is not to suggest that there's any distance here, a single line that feels academic (though it has all been magnificently researched) or at emotive remove. Mondor's passion for those days and those people, her intimate knowing, is galvanizing. She's tough, and she's been toughened; she rarely puts her own self center stage. But when she appears, when she tells us something personal, the stories stick.

HOUSE OF STONE: A MEMOIR OF HOME, FAMILY, AND A LOST MIDDLE EAST/Anthony Shadid

House of Stone is breathtaking—gigantic in ambition, equal to that ambition, combustible and yet right in its mix of country history, imagined (or imaginatively *supplemented*) familial history, personal yearning, poetry, politics, and passion flowers. It recounts the months Anthony Shadid spent rebuilding his great-grandfather's estate in old Marjayoun. It gives us Shadid, newly divorced and with a daughter far away, seeking to resurrect the idea of home. It introduces the sarcasm and suspicions and ironies and odd camaraderie of a band of Lebanese neighbors and fickle house builders. It memorializes a dying doctor who knows everything, it seems, about gardens. A book built of many parts, *House* yet works, sweeping foreigners like myself toward its quiet, exotic heart. There is war, and there is the pickling of olives. There is dust, yet flowers grow. There are age-old accusations and cautions about war. There is a father working so far from the daughter he loves but choosing to believe in days yet to come. There is Shadid's own sadness over those who have died too soon—by horse, by weakened lungs. Yes, horse. Yes, weakened lungs. It is nearly unbearable to read these passages, but they are so beautiful and holy that we do.

NO HEROES: A MEMOIR OF COMING HOME/ Chris Offutt

Chris Offutt's memoir is an odd composite—a gloriously funny and moving account of the year the author returned to his Kentucky roots to teach at his alma mater, interspersed with the stories of his parents-in-law, two Holocaust survivors. What binds the two narratives—more or less—is Offutt's desire to try to locate home, or at least to define it. What makes this memoir such a compelling read is Offutt's mastery of voice. Ironic, sardonic, ultimately tenderhearted Kentucky twang lives on every page of this book. Simple sentences. Walkabout sounds. Startling, original images that keep a reader reading.

HIROSHIMA IN THE MORNING/ Rahna Reiko Rizzuto

When Rahna Reiko Rizzuto wins a grant that will take her to Japan for six months to complete research for a book, everything changes. She'll be leaving her husband and two toddler boys at home. She'll be entering a new landscape, be forced to negotiate, at least somewhat, in the language of her ancestors. She leaves New York City as a professional on a quest. She arrives in Japan as a woman with unprecedented freedoms. Everything can be questioned in this environment, and everything is. What is a mother? What is a wife? What is owed, and what must be taken? Whose side do we stand on when the question is survival? Built of letters, interview transcripts, travelogue entries, and questions of responsibility to self and others, *Hiroshima in the Morning* wades into dangerous, even inflammatory territory and rocks easy assumptions about sacrifice and selfishness: "It is a question of time, and time is the question: How does one spend it? When does the part about living your life to the fullest begin to shift into just making do, and then into suffering, and how do any of us know where we are in this process?"

NOTHING TO DECLARE: MEMOIRS OF A WOMAN TRAVELING ALONE/Mary Morris

I traveled to San Miguel because of this book—because of the way it introduced me to a landscape, a culture, a desire. Mary Morris is young, on her own, and searching when she sets off for a journey south. She must choose what to trust and who to be as she interacts with strangers and strange places. This is an expat tale. It is also beautiful writing about remembering: "Women remember. Our bodies remember. Every part of us remembers everything that has ever happened. Every touch, every feel, everything is there in our skin, ready to be awakened, revived. . . . The water entered me and I could not tell where my body stopped and the sea began. My body was gone, but all the remembering was there."

RAPACIOUS MINDS

ISTANBUL: MEMORIES AND THE CITY/Orhan Pamuk

Some memoirs wind you back through the crowded streets of the hero's childhood. Some wend you through the neural pathways of the author's craving, omnivorous mind. *Istanbul*, by the Nobel Prize–winning Orhan Pamuk, does both. Sebaldian in scope, suffused with gorgeous black-and-white photographs of historic Istanbul, this is an exploration of a city, a man, and a particularly rich, involving melancholic state known as *hüzün*. "The *hüzün* of Istanbul is not just the mood evoked by its music and its poetry," writes Pamuk, "it is a way of looking at life that implicates us all, not only a spiritual state but a state of mind that is ultimately as life-affirming as it is negating." *Istanbul* sprawls like the city sprawls. Its sentences can sometimes consume entire pages as they evoke landscapes and childhood rooms, gossip and history, painters and writers. Pamuk takes readers on a journey—his journey—as a boy in love with his mother, as a teen in love with his city, and as a young man who ultimately chooses writing over painting. Pamuk is tenderly and brilliantly tortured. He is obsessed with ruins and all the loss that ruins imply.

NOTHING TO BE FRIGHTENED OF/ Julian Barnes

This is a helpful meditation on death and dying—on how people die (which is, of course, bound up with how people live) and on what people think along the way. Fear or acceptance? Defeat or glory? Ungainly irony or something worse? It is only partly memoir; it's equal parts wit and philosophy and literary biography. It's a chapterless not–outright diatribe, not–clinical exploration—perhaps *controlled rant* is the term—that is nothing if not (and you know this matters to me) brilliantly choreographed. Julian Barnes assaults you. He appeases you. He is on your side and then he's all caught up with himself, as if he may be the only one facing ultimate extinction. No such luck, Barnes. It's a privilege to watch a mind like Barnes's work over, around, and through the inexplicableness of death. It's exhilarating, as a matter of fact, and has much to teach to true memoir writers.

A STEP FROM DEATH: A MEMOIR/
Larry Woiwode

Perhaps the hardest books to write are those that hold themselves accountable to no conventional boundaries or forms. Those that permit time to spill across their pages—backward, forward, a rush of movement, a sudden stilling, returns and retreats. Those in which one thought juts deeply into the core of another, in which elisions are story, in which one is at a loss to define a true end or beginning. Books like these cannot hold their readers, let alone survive themselves, unless they are perfectly calibrated—orchestrated as if by some higher power so that all the fragments do at last become a gleaming, self-sustaining whole. Regrets, wants, self-disgust, confessions—all of that is here in the mad, bold waters of this book. But *A Step from Death* is meant to be so much more than that: a reconciliation with self, a bid to understand fathers and fatherhood. It tumbles and stonewalls and enthralls and wounds, roping readers through the thick braid of its sentences, its unapologetic instructions on how to read the book. One senses no precocity here, no purposeful manipulations. One senses, instead, a struggle to find the best way to say the hardest things, to put a life into context.

UNCLE TUNGSTEN: MEMORIES OF A CHEMICAL BOYHOOD/Oliver Sacks

I like to remind my students, every now and then, that one need not have had a childhood of hardship or terror, high adventure or deprivation to have within one the stuff of memoir. Oliver Sacks's quiet but lovely *Uncle Tungsten* is a case in point. "Many of my childhood memories are of metals: these seemed to exert a power on me from the start," the book begins. "They stood out, conspicuous against the heterogeneousness of the world, by their shining, gleaming quality, their silveriness, their smoothness and weight. They seemed cool to the touch, and they rang when they were struck." Passion, then—its emergence, its evolution, its effect on the shape of a life—lies at the core of this book, the discovery and nurturing of one boy's purpose.

ALL THE STRANGE HOURS: THE EXCAVATION OF A LIFE/Loren Eiseley

By his own admission, Loren Eiseley appears "to know nothing of what I truly am: gambler, scholar, or fugitive." By external measures he was an archaeologist, an acclaimed author, a teacher at my own University of Pennsylvania and elsewhere. *All the Strange Hours*, first published in 1975 and written in the late years of Eiseley's life, is a stunning attempt at reconciling the many fragments of his wildly variant experiences as the son of a harsh deaf woman, a young man riding the rails during the Great Depression, an archaeologist, and a writer in the making. His text melds memories vital and true. It blends visions and fears. Eiseley demonstrates an acute talent for finding meaning in landscape. He is brilliant on time. He has a striking gift for describing people. He writes sentences like these: "Oncoming age is to me a vast wild autumn country strewn with broken seedpods, hurrying cloud wrack, abandoned farm machinery, and circling crows. A place where things were begun on too grand a scale to complete."

FUNNY BUSINESS

Memoir—the life recalled and sifted not just for the sake of narrative but also for the sake of some transcendent knowing—isn't always an easy fit for humorists, who naturally gravitate toward fish stories and flights of fancy, hyperbole and all varieties of magnification. Sometimes—often—funny lives in the overestimated, the caricature, the stretch. Sometimes extreme coagulation or tricked-out inventory is the place where laughter starts. Short and to the point is frequently more effective than long, cohering, and flowy. Punch lines have been known to trounce epiphanies.

Humor memoirs, then, aren't always actual memoirs, but who doesn't want to laugh? My students often ask me what to do with their real-life funny stuff. When they do, I point them to these books.

A GIRL NAMED ZIPPY: GROWING UP SMALL IN MOORELAND, INDIANA/Haven Kimmel

Wielding a perfectly calibrated child's voice and reporting on her hometown of a mere 300 strange nonstrangers, Haven Kimmel never lets her foot off the funny pedal in *A Girl*

Named Zippy. It's all gullibility and incredulity—one or the other, sometimes both at the same time. It's *what's going on here?* ruminations on bad hair, chicken love, familial disputes, improbable alliances, odd neighbors, and bad card games. It's a wry science-fiction-loving mother, a deal-making father, a perfect sister (except when she isn't), and a very tall brother who turns out to be quite smart. And then there are all those neighbors. Kimmel makes us laugh without implicating us in ridicule. She writes lines like these about her famously unruly hair: "The really short haircut (the Pixie, as it was then called) was my favorite, and coincidentally, the most hideous. Many large, predatory birds believed I was asking for a date."

A WALK IN THE WOODS: REDISCOVERING AMERICA ON THE APPALACHIAN TRAIL/Bill Bryson

I'm not sure Bill Bryson would slot this memoiristic travelogue into the Funny Business pages of *Handling the Truth*, but I do because of this: One night, sleepless, I grabbed *A Walk in the Woods*, curled up on the couch, and then proceeded to fall to the floor twice thanks to uncontrollable laughter. I'd bought the book out of curiosity about the Appalachian Trail and the Great Smoky Mountains National Park, which my great-grandfather Horace Kephart helped to create. I'd hoped to learn about geology and last chances for an essential wilderness. Bryson delivers that, of course, along with wit, history, and regional color, making this a trail adventure with a non-self-glorifying greater purpose. But Bryson is also consistently hilarious, as with this description of his sidekick, Katz: "His posture brought to mind a shipwreck victim clinging to a square of floating wreckage on rough seas, or possibly someone who had been lifted unexpectedly into the sky on top of a weather balloon he was preparing to hoist—in any case, someone holding on for dear life in dangerous circumstances."

BOSSYPANTS/Tina Fey

I read *Bossypants* with an odd sense of *You go, girl* familiarity. Or maybe the pride I was feeling was pride in my own gender—the smartness of Tina Fey, the intelligence of her voice, the fluidity of her prose, the sense you get that she wrote this whole thing on her own, without the intercession of a hired pen. In *Bossypants*, we get the down and dirty on Fey's growing up, her funny friends, her appealing parents. We see Fey at work as a young comedienne, as a young comedic writer, as the supernova force behind *30 Rock*. Amid all that is so funny, all that sings so smoothly along, we get Fey as the non-Celeb celebrity. She's just a person—kinda like you, kinda like me. She's wowed by her good fortune, she's annoyed by her critics, she's amused by Photoshopping, and she's not going to judge your parenting style, even if you choose to judge hers. It is by connecting with her readers—by reaching across what might have been the great divide—that Fey delivers memoir.

ME TALK PRETTY ONE DAY/David Sedaris

Shortly after I started reading David Sedaris's *Me Talk Pretty One Day*, I started meeting the author in my dreams. It's true. There he'd be, wielding a purple feather duster and reviving a poignant, painful moment from his past—something, say, about his youthful ambitions to be a commercial jingle singer. A few nights later, I'd meet up with Sedaris again—this time in a Parisian café, where he'd regale me with tales of his many troubles learning the oversexed French language from an impatient instructor. I'd find myself waking up sore-throated and exhausted, the taste of the dream-induced laughter still on my tongue. Sedaris has been called a modern-day Mark Twain and Garrison Keillor's evil twin. He's been likened to J. D. Salinger and Dorothy Parker. But in fact he is an unassuming original, a middle-aged guy who remembers all too well how it felt to be young and gay and obsessed and inadequate, and whose acute vulnerability springboards his writing even now. Occasionally bawdy, giddily obscene, perpetually on the lookout for foibles and flaws, Sedaris somehow never fails to finally respect his subject matter. His sharp tongue achieves acuity, not cruelty. His humor pokes but never skewers.

WHY I'M LIKE THIS: TRUE STORIES/Cynthia Kaplan

Comprising twenty-one short tales, *Why I'm Like This* begins with a hilarious send-up of Cynthia Kaplan's final year at "Queechy Lake Camp" and ends with a tour de force about the cruelly unfulfilled lives of truffle pigs. In between, we meet Kaplan's father, the unrepentant "Gadgeteer"; Kaplan's mother, who hopes against hope that the author will some-day learn fashion; Kaplan's husband, who rescues Kaplan from a lifetime of loser boyfriends; Kaplan's pill-popping, self-absorbed, and disturbingly untidy therapist; Kaplan's wide-eyed newborn son; and, most touchingly, Kaplan's grandparents. In tale after tale, Kaplan yields fragments of a life, torn-out episodes, scrupulously polished set pieces that rise above their punch lines to achieve not just humor but also poignancy. Both honest and compassionate, refreshingly intelligent, fastidiously articulate, Kaplan writes not at the expense of others but at the expense of herself. Never the most popular girl in the class, often lonely, frequently waking up with the wrong kind of man, afraid of moths—afraid, indeed, of most things—Kaplan is all too aware of her conflicted dark side, her own desperate, fatalistic, worrisome, worrying self. With her unique brand of humane observation and wit, with her deadpan voice and her fearless honesty, Kaplan's book is one in which people will recognize some heretofore unearthed part of their own history or selves.

HELPFUL TEXTS

THE SITUATION AND THE STORY: THE ART OF PERSONAL NARRATIVE/Vivian Gornick

Vivian Gornick's *The Situation and the Story* provides students (and teachers) with a broadened understanding of the task ahead. Writers of memoir, says Gornick, must develop a persona, must identify the telling situation(s), and must, essentially, locate the story inside the situation—the reason the situation matters, the why of it all. I frequently introduce Gornick into my lessons. I find that when I do, students begin to look at their own work and say, *Well, yes, I've described my situation brilliantly (perhaps), but I have no idea, still, what my story is.* Beyond Gornick's ideology lie her fascinating, in-depth assessments of many classic memoirs.

I COULD TELL YOU STORIES: SOJOURNS IN THE LAND OF MEMORY/Patricia Hampl

I never teach the same thing twice, but that doesn't mean I forsake the classics in favor of novelty. The one essay that I have carried forward into every memoir class is Patricia

Hampl's "Memory and Imagination," found within *I Could Tell You Stories*. You just don't teach memoir without it, or at least I don't. You can't go far without words such as these:

> We seek a means of exchange, a language which will renew these ancient concerns and make them wholly, pulsingly ours. Instinctively, we go to our store of private associations for our authority to speak of these weighty issues. We find, in our details and broken, obscured images, the language of symbol. Here memory impulsively reaches out and embraces imagination. That is the resort to invention. It isn't a lie, but an act of necessity, as the innate urge to locate truth always is.

Hampl believes that "the narrative self (the culprit who invented) wishes to be discovered by the reflective self, the self who wants to understand and make sense of a half-remembered moment about a nun sneezing in the sun."

VANISHING POINT: NOT
A MEMOIR/Ander Monson

Ander Monson's *The Vanishing Point* is interesting stuff—quotable, inventive, daggered, asterisked, *me*-dominated and *me*-avoidant, not quite memoir, though Monson himself would be the first to count all the sentences beginning with (or featuring) that single letter *I*. Monson is full of rue and half steps, full of self-disclosures that may or may not reveal the actual self. Full, most of all, of the questions: *Can the actual self be revealed? Can the we be known? Is the I a reliable story?* Monson is thinking out loud, in these pages, about truths and dares, about how the technology we write with may or may not shape what we write. He is thinking about solipsisms and (magnificently) "assembloirs," and he gets us thinking, too. Playfully, insistently, self-defeatedly, self-aggrandizingly, Monson puts a lot at stake.

THE ART OF TIME IN MEMOIR:
THEN, AGAIN/Sven Birkerts

With quiet intelligence, Sven Birkerts begins *The Art of Time in Memoir* with a story about his own descent into the making of memoir. What did the memories he had ready access to mean? How were involuntary memories leading him away from the obvious "events" of his life toward a braided understanding of his life's meaning? What could the memoirs of Annie Dillard, Frank Conroy, Jo Ann Beard, Paul Auster, Virginia Woolf, and so many others teach? Birkerts is a first-rate critic. His reflections on classic memoirs are, I think, unparalleled, and his obsession with time is instructive. Finally, for those who remain unconvinced that there is a real and important difference between memoir and autobiography, Birkerts provides the best clarification I've seen. I'll quote at length here, because it matters. Autobiography, Birkerts begins by telling us, is "the line of one's own life." Memoirs,

> by contrast are neither open ended nor
> provisional. For as the root of the word
> attests, they present not the line of the life
> but the life remembered. They are pledged

not to an ostensibly detached accounting of events but to presentation of life as it is narratively reconstituted by memory. The memoirist is generally not after the sequenced account of his life so much as the story or stories that have given that life its internal shape.

THE MADE-UP SELF: IMPERSONATION IN THE PERSONAL ESSAY/Carl H. Klaus

If the titles designating the four parts of this slender paperback seem, at first, daunting—"Evocations of Consciousness," "Evocations of Personality," "Personae and Culture," and "Personae and Personal Experience"—there's a lot of good stuff in between. Ruminations on the poetics of self, the possibility/impossibility of tracking the mind at work, the grand seductions and sometimes promise of what Carl Klaus, the founding director of the University of Iowa's Nonfiction Writing Program, calls "the literature of interiority. The story of thought. The drama of mind in action," etc. We get satisfying reflections on Montaigne reflecting on Montaigne, pithy quotes from nonfiction masters, mind teases that force us to conclude (again and again) that writing (and reading) the personal essay is both a minefield and an irresistible enterprise. The personal essay and memoir are cousins, or can be. There are puzzles worth de-puzzling here.

MEMOIR: A HISTORY/Ben Yagoda

Reason number one to read Ben Yagoda's *Memoir: A History*: You'll learn something about the wherefore and comeuppance of the personal story (I use the term *personal story* because Yagoda devotes a considerable percentage of his book to autobiography, which is not—see Birkerts above—precisely the same as memoir). Reason number two: You'll steel yourself for many of the assaults that are now directed at this nervy enterprise. Yagoda's sweep through the generations touches on such disparate characters as Augustine, Rousseau, Ulysses S. Grant, Mark Twain, Helen Keller, Kathryn Harrison, and James Frey. It offers an up-to-date survey of the scientific work that debunks the possibility of foolproof remembered truth. Yagoda has fun cataloging memoir's many crimes. Still, he does, in the end, confess that the memoir boom "has been a net plus for the cause of writing."

ON WRITING: A MEMOIR
OF THE CRAFT/Stephen King

Years ago, when my son was in sixth grade, I lay on his narrow bed while he sat propped up on the floor, reading aloud from Stephen King's *On Writing*. You would have thought we were reading some extraterrestrial, action-jammed tale the way we returned to this book each day, for that's the kind of book this is—the kind that you can't get enough of. It's King's personal writing tale, and in it he generously imparts lessons about what to write and where to write it; narration, description, and dialogue; drafting and redrafting; and just about anything else writers need to know to write well. Writers in any genre would benefit from reading this book. Memoirists, by extension, will, too.

BIRD BY BIRD: SOME INSTRUCTIONS
ON WRITING AND LIFE/Anne Lamott

Finally, but of course, there's Anne Lamott's *Bird by Bird*. Wily, funny, honest, wholly empathetic, and self-confessional, this, like King's book, is designed for those working in any genre, meaning that there's plenty here for memoirists. Short assignments, perfectionism, morality, broccoli, jealousy—they're all here not just for the taking but also for the applying.

SOME ADDITIONALLY CITED SOURCES

Anonymous, *A Woman in Berlin: Eight Weeks in the Conquered City—A Diary*

Susannah Cahalan, *Brain on Fire: My Month of Madness*

Elias Canetti, *The Tongue Set Free*

Teresa Carpenter, editor, *New York Diaries: 1609 to 2009*

Leah Hager Cohen, *Train Go Sorry: Inside a Deaf World*

Terrence Des Pres, "Writing into the World" and "Accident and Its Scene: Reflections on the Death of John Gardner"

Joan Didion, "On Keeping a Notebook"

Dave Eggers, *A Heartbreaking Work of Staggering Genius*

Forrest Gander, *As a Friend: A Novel*

Elizabeth Gilbert, *Eat, Pray, Love: One Woman's Search for Everything Across Italy, India and Indonesia*

Priscilla Gilman, *The Anti-Romantic Child: A Memoir of Unexpected Joy*

Natalia Ginzburg, "My Craft"

Francisco Goldman, *Say Her Name: A Novel*

Ted Kooser, "Applesauce"

Jenny Lawson, *Let's Petend This Never Happened: A Mostly True Memoir*

Chang-rae Lee, "Coming Home Again"

Debra Marquart, *The Horizontal World: Growing Up Wild in the Middle of Nowhere*

J. R. Moehringer, *The Tender Bar: A Memoir*

Kate Moses, *Cakewalk: A Memoir*

Azar Nafisi, *Reading Lolita in Tehran: A Memoir in Books*

Nasdijj, *The Boy and the Dog Are Sleeping*

Pablo Neruda, *Absence and Presence*

Joyce Carol Oates, *A Widow's Story: A Memoir*

Nuala O'Faolain, *Are You Somebody?: The Accidental Memoir of a Dublin Woman*

Alice Ozma, *The Reading Promise: My Father and the Books We Shared*

Lia Purpura, *"Autopsy Report"*

Rainer Maria Rilke, *Letters to a Young Poet*

Jane Satterfield, *Daughters of Empire: A Memoir of a Year in Britain and Beyond*

Gerald Stern, "Eggshell"

Sallie Tisdale, "Violation"

Eudora Welty, *One Writer's Beginnings*

Virginia Woolf, *A Room of One's Own*

ACKNOWLEDGMENTS

I begin with the students. All of the students. The youngest ones, who years ago came first to my house and then to a garden, with exhilarating faith in stories. The faraway ones, in Maryland and California, in Wisconsin. The ones whom I met for just a morning or an afternoon, the ones who added me to their rosters and stayed. Students teach the teachers how, and I have been outrageously blessed in my lessons. I have, over and again, fallen in love. For the questions asked, for the memories written, for the saturating joy of each one of you, unquantifiable thanks. To those who generously share their beauty here—Andrea Amanullah, Leah Apple, Rachel Au-Yong, Dascher Branch-Elliman, Kimberly Eisler, Katie Goldrath, Sara Kalkstein, Elizabeth Knight, Nabil Mehta, Erin Nigro, Jonathan Packer, Joseph Polin, Beryl Sanders, Gabriel Seidner, and Stephanie C. Trott—I am honored to carry your words forward.

Thank you to Gregory Djanikian, Al Filreis, and Mingo Reynolds, who have made room for me at the University of Pennsylvania, and to Greg, especially, for the conversation.

Thank you to Karen Rile, my indispensable and talented colleague at Penn, and to Alyson Hagy, Ivy Goodman, Lisa Zeidner, Rahna Reiko Rizzuto, and Elizabeth Mosier—exemplary writers and teachers and abiding friends who have been there, in so many ways, throughout this teaching journey. Thank you to Kelly Simmons, who calls when I need to laugh, or cry, and to Colleen Mondor and Katrina Kenison for the dialogue.

Thank you to Melissa Sarno, who, in an awesomely clever response to one of my occasional Facebook tirades about a certain non-memoir memoir, passed along a YouTube clip from an early Aaron Sorkin movie. And so a title was born.

Thank you to Elizabeth Taylor at the *Chicago Tribune*, John Prendergast at the *Pennsylvania Gazette,* Michael Pakenham formerly of *Baltimore Sun,* Karen Templer formerly of *Readerville*, as well as the editors of the *Philadelphia Inquirer*, the *Washington Post*, *Book* magazine, *Philadelphia* magazine*, Salon,* the *New York Times*, *Shelf Awareness*, *Publishing Perspectives*, *Publishers Weekly,* and elsewhere, who have, through the years, given me room to write about books and the book life. Some of the books referenced in *Handling the Truth* first made their way to me for review thanks to these editors, and at times, I borrow heavily from myself. It was a gift to appear first in your publications.

Thank you to the bloggers who, with outrageous generosity, have supported this writing dream of mine, and who have given me cause, every single day, to wake up and think and blog forward. Some of what appears in *Handling the Truth* first appeared, in different form, on my blog. I have been enlightened and heartened by the conversation.

Thank you to the great memoirists, so many of them cited here, who have inspired, goaded, appeased, and made the world a smarter, gentler, more interesting place. Some of them are my enduring friends. These friendships matter hugely.

Thank you to William Shinker for his warm welcome to the fabulous Gotham Books. Thank you to Lauren Marino, my Gotham editor, for her immediate embrace of this book, for her great good humor, for her guiding touch, and for her friendship along the way. I would not have wanted to publish this book with any other. Thank you to Susan Barnes for all the big and small things I know you do, and for the sprightly e-mail conversations. Thank you to Mary Beth Constant, copy editor supreme, who took such deep interest, who read so closely, who saved me from my fast-typing self, who opined, and who made me laugh; your contribution to these pages is priceless. Thank you to Mimi Barke, who produced a timeless, original, and (I think) striking image for the cover of this book; I will be so proud to have this prettily outfitted thing sit on my shelf. Thank you to Spring Hoteling, who made this book so gorgeous, page by page, and to Lavina Lee, Erica Ferguson, and Dora Mak, who brought such care to the production process. Thank you to Beth Parker, Gotham publicist, who understood at once what mattered most about this book, and who generously made sure that others did as well. Thank you to Lisa Johnson and Jessica Chun, who so passionately launched this book into the world. Thank you to my first Penguin family—Tamra Tuller, Michael Green, Jessica Shoffel, and Jill Santopolo—for believing in my work, and in me, and for shoring up the foundations of my writing life.

Thank you—thank you—to Amy Rennert, who received this book on a Saturday and called me the very next day, a Sunday, certain. Shortly thereafter (a mere snap in time), Amy was calling to say that this book had found its perfect Gotham home. These are the calls a writer never forgets, and for her unflagging support of this book, for knowing how much these students mean to me, for understanding why I had to overtly handle truth—make these confessions, offer these cautions—thank you. And thanks, too, to Robyn Russell, for all the years.

Finally, I was a student at the University of Pennsylvania primarily because my father had been a student there before me. This learning life of mine begins, then, with him. Living itself would not be possible without the two men who rock my world: my husband, Bill, and our son, Jeremy. Countless times, over the past many years, I have consulted with my bright and beautiful son about living and about teaching. Always he has known what to say. When I have doubted myself, when I have regretted, when I have wanted to pull some of my own pages back, when I haven't trusted that my process would hold, Jeremy—pure-hearted and absolute, bedrock in his conviction that when our words can help others, we should use them, smarter than anyone I know—has stood firm. I am a teacher because I was a mother first. I am lucky in this life.

ABOUT THE AUTHOR

William Robert Sulit

Beth Kephart, a National Book Award finalist, is the author of five memoirs. Her other books include the autobiography of Philadelphia's Schuylkill River, *Flow*; the Spring 2010 IndieBound Pick *The Heart Is Not a Size*; the Autumn 2010 IndieBound Pick *Dangerous Neighbors*; and the critically acclaimed novels for young adults *Undercover, House of Dance, Nothing But Ghosts, You Are My Only*, and *Small Damages*. Kephart is a winner of the Pennsylvania Council on the Arts fiction grant, a National Endowment for the Arts grant, a Leeway grant, a Pew Fellowships in the Arts grant, and the Speakeasy Poetry Prize, among other honors. Her essays are frequently anthologized, she has judged many competitions, she has written for numerous national magazines and newspapers, and she has taught workshops across the United States, to all ages. Kephart teaches creative nonfiction at the University of Pennsylvania and served as the inaugural readergirlz author-in-residence. She is the strategic writing partner in the boutique marketing communications firm Fusion. In 2014 Chronicle Books will release *Going Over.* Please visit Beth's blog, twice named a top author blog during Book Blogger Appreciation Week, at www.beth-kephart.blogspot.com.